MW01285667

# Instant Pot Vortex Plus Air Fryer Oven Cookbook

*2000-Day Quick and Easy Recipe with Healthy and Delicious Fried and Baked Meals for Beginners and Advanced Users*

Tim Yaeml

© Copyright 2021 Tim Yaeml- All Rights Reserved.

In no way is it legal to reproduce, duplicate, or transmit any part of this document by either electronic means or in printed format. Recording of this publication is strictly prohibited, and any storage of this material is not allowed unless with written permission from the publisher. All rights reserved.

The information provided herein is stated to be truthful and consistent, in that any liability, regarding inattention or otherwise, by any usage or abuse of any policies, processes, or directions contained within is the solitary and complete responsibility of the recipient reader. Under no circumstances will any legal liability or blame be held against the publisher for any reparation, damages, or monetary loss due to the information herein, either directly or indirectly.

Respective authors own all copyrights not held by the publisher.

**Legal Notice:**

This book is copyright protected. This is only for personal use. You cannot amend, distribute, sell, use, quote or paraphrase any part of the content within this book without the consent of the author or copyright owner. Legal action will be pursued if this is breached.

**Disclaimer Notice:**

Please note the information contained within this document is for educational and entertainment purposes only. Every attempt has been made to provide accurate, up-to-date and reliable, complete information. No warranties of any kind are expressed or implied. Readers acknowledge that the author is not engaging in the rendering of legal, financial, medical or professional advice.

By reading this document, the reader agrees that under no circumstances are we responsible for any losses, direct or indirect, which are incurred as a result of the use of information contained within this document, including, but not limited to, errors, omissions, or inaccuracies.

# Table of Contents

# Introduction

Air frying is gaining more popularity by the day for its uniqueness to create crispy, healthy foods that play down on excess oil consumption when frying; hence, a wide range of single-functioned air fryers on the market. The Instant Pot Vortex Plus air fryer oven changes things a bit. It comes along as not only supporting the use of air frying for cooking but also combines the entire function of the oven.

This hearty collection of hand-picked high-quality recipes to suit all tastes and needs. All the ingredients are affordable and locally sourced from local stores. And many recipes take care of your previous time in the kitchen. Perfect for cutting the hassle and stress at mealtime. From the book, you will not only find flavorful recipes, but also find hot tips and tricks on how to use your Instant Pot Vortex Plus air fryer oven .

# Chapter 1: Instant Pot Vortex Plus Air Fryer Oven Basics

## Instant Pot Vortex Plus Air Fryer Oven

The Instant Pot Vortex Plus Air Fryer Oven is one of the most advanced multi cooking appliances available in the market now. The biggest advantage of the vortex air fryer oven is that its large 10-quart capacity. It is capable to cook a large number of foods at once. Instant Pot Vortex Plus Air Fryer Oven is 7-in-1 multipurpose smart cooking appliances run on advanced microprocessor technology. It not only saves your kitchen space but also performs various cooking tasks into a single appliance. The smart programs are preset and design to get a perfect cooking result every time. Using these programs, you can easily air-fry crispy French fries, bake your favorite cakes and cookies, roast whole chicken at a time, broil fish or meat, reheat your leftover food and also dehydrate your favorite veggies and fruit slices. It is one of the best replacement options for your microwave, oven, dehydrator, and toaster.

The Instant Pot Vortex Plus Air Fryer Oven comes with a user-friendly control system easily operates by anyone. No special skill requires operating your vortex air fryer oven. Just follow the instruction manual and cook healthy and delicious dishes at home. It cooks your food by circulating very hot air into the cooking chamber with the help of a convection fan. This will give you faster and even cooking results. It deep-fries your food into very less oil without compromising the taste and texture of deep-fried food. This will help to reduce your daily calorie consumption and make healthier and tasty dishes easily.

## How Instant Pot Vortex Plus Air Fryer Oven Works?

The instant vortex air fryer requires 1500-watt energy and it is capable to produce a high temperature of 400° F. It works similarly as the convection oven technology. It uses hot air circulation technology in which very hot dry heats are circulating with the help of a convection fan around the food basket to cook your food fast and evenly from all the sides.

The instant vortex air fryer comes with 6 different accessories which help to make your daily cooking process easy. These accessories are 2 no's of Cooking Tray, Drip Pan, Rotisserie Basket, Rotisserie split with settings screw, 2 no's of rotisserie fork, and rotisserie lift. Before starting the actual cooking, process makes sure your instant vortex air fryer is kept on a flat surface.

- If preheat is require then preheat your vortex air fryer oven before placing the food inside. It takes approximately 3 to 4 minutes to preheat the air fryer oven.
- When the oven reaches the target temperature then the display indicates **Add Food**. Use hand protection gloves while placing your food into the cooking tray carefully and close the door.
- As per recipe requirements if the display indicates **turn Food** then turn, flip and shake the food.
- After finishing the cooking process display indicates **End** which means that the current running smart program has ended.

## Buttons and Functions of Instant Pot Vortex Plus Air Fryer Oven

The vortex air fryer oven has various smart functions and buttons which makes your daily cooking simple and easy.

### Touch Panel Display

The Instant Pot Vortex Plus Air Fryer Oven comes with a big touch panel display. The display panel is equipped with automatic smart function and manual settings. The display helps to know the currently running programs, cooking time, cooking temperature, remainders, and error messages. When the air fryer oven is on standby mode then the display reads *OFF*.

### Smart Functions

The vortex air fryer oven has equipped with smart functions, these functions are loaded with preset settings. While using these smart functions you never worry about time and temperature settings.

- **Air Fry:** Using this function you can air fry your favorite fried food into very less oil. A bowl of French fries requires just a tablespoon of oil to fry into an air fryer oven. It makes your French fries crispy from outside and tender from inside.
- **Roast:** Using rotisserie accessories you can roast your favorite meat, chicken, and beef under this function. Due to the 10-quart size, you can easily roast a whole chicken at a time.
- **Broil:** This function works similarly as grilling it helps to brown or toasting your food under direct radiant heat.

- **Bake:** This function is used to bake your favorite cakes, cookies, and desserts.
- **Reheat:** Using this function you can reheat pastries, frozen, and leftover food again.
- **Dehydrate:** This function allows you to dehydrate lots of food at once. It allows you to dehydrate your favorite fruits, vegetables, and meat slices.

## Temp (+/-)

This function is used to adjust the temperature setting manually as per your recipe needs by pressing (+/-).

## Time (+/-)

This function is used to adjust the time setting manually as per your recipe needs by processing (+/-).

## Rotate

Once the cooking process is running you can use the rotate function to on and off the rotation of the rotisserie. This function is used while roasting your food.

## Light

Using this function, you can see your food while cooking. Touching this function will ON and OFF the oven light. The light is automatically off after 2 minutes.

## Cancel

Using this button, you can stop the current running program. While pressing this button the display reads OFF and the oven automatically goes into standby mode.

## Start

This button is used to start the actual cooking process.

# Benefits of Vortex Air Fryer Oven

The instant vortex air fryer has magical multi-cooking appliances that come with various benefits. These benefits include

### 1. Requires less oil to cook your food

Compare to the traditional deep-frying method vortex air fryer requires very little oil to fry your food. It requires 85 % less oil compared with another deep-frying method. It fries your French fries within a tablespoon of oil without changing the taste and texture like deep-fried food. It makes your French fries crisp from outside and tender from inside.

## 2. Saves cooking time

Instant Pot Vortex Plus Air Fryer Oven is cooking your food by circulating very hot air into the cooking chamber. It blows 400° F hot air to cook your food very fast and it helps to save you cooking time. If you are one of the people who have a busy schedule, then the vortex air fryer oven is the best kitchen gadget for you. It cooks food faster and gives even cooking results within very less time.

## 3. Multi-cooking appliance

Vortex air fryer is one of the multi cooking appliances and the best replacement for microwave, oven, toaster, and dehydrator. It performs the task of the different appliances into a single cooking appliance. Due to this it not only saves your kitchen countertop space but also saves your money.

## 4. Smart cooking programs

Instant vortex air fryer loaded with smart cooking functions. It includes Air fry, Roast, Dehydrate, Reheat, Bake, and Broil. All these functions are pre-programmed, and you can use these functions without worrying about time and temperature settings.

## 5. Safe appliance to use

The vortex air fryer oven has come with a built-in protection feature against overheating. If the oven temperature exceeds over 450° F then the appliance is automatically shut off and the display reads error message E2.

# Chapter 2: Breakfast & Brunch Recipes

## Baked Eggs

Preparation Time: 10 minutes

Cooking Time: 15 minutes

Serve: 2

**Ingredients:**

- 4 eggs
- 2 tbsp cheddar cheese, shredded
- 4 tbsp butter, melted

**Directions:**

1. Divide melted butter into the two ramekins.
2. Drop 2 eggs into each ramekin and top with 1 tbsp cheddar cheese.
3. Select BAKE mode, then set the temperature to 350 F and the time to 15 minutes, then press start.
4. When the display shows Add Food then place ramekins on the cooking tray and place in the vortex plus air fryer oven.
5. Serve and enjoy.

**Nutritional Value (Amount per Serving):**

- Calories 358
- Fat 34.1 g
- Carbohydrates 0.8 g
- Sugar 0.7 g
- Protein 13.1 g
- Cholesterol 369 mg

# Zucchini Breakfast Quiche

Preparation Time: 10 minutes

Cooking Time: 40 minutes

Serve: 6

**Ingredients:**

- 8 eggs
- 1 cup zucchini, shredded and squeeze out all liquid
- 1/2 cup heavy cream
- 1 cup cheddar cheese, shredded
- 1/2 cup ham, cooked and diced
- 1/2 tsp dry mustard
- Pepper
- Salt

**Directions:**

1. Mix together zucchini, cheddar cheese, and ham in a greased baking dish.
2. In a bowl, whisk together eggs, heavy cream, mustard, pepper, and salt. Pour egg mixture over the zucchini mixture.
3. Select BAKE mode, then set the temperature to 375 F and the time to 40 minutes, then press start.
4. When the display shows Add Food then place the baking dish in the vortex plus air fryer oven.
5. Serve and enjoy.

**Nutritional Value (Amount per Serving):**

- Calories 217
- Fat 16.9 g
- Carbohydrates 2.1 g
- Sugar 0.9 g
- Protein 14.5 g
- Cholesterol 258 mg

# Poppyseed Breakfast Muffins

Preparation Time: 10 minutes

Cooking Time: 40 minutes

Serve: 12

**Ingredients:**

- 3 eggs
- 2 tbsp poppy seeds
- 1/4 cup coconut oil
- 1/4 cup ricotta cheese
- 1 cup almond flour
- 1 tsp lemon extract
- 1/4 cup heavy cream
- 4 true lemon packets
- 1 tsp baking powder
- 1/3 cup Truvia

**Directions:**

1. Add all ingredients into the large bowl and beat until fluffy.
2. Pour egg mixture into the 12 silicone muffin molds.
3. Select BAKE mode, then set the temperature to 350 F and the time to 40 minutes, then press start.
4. When the display shows Add Food then place muffin molds on the cooking tray and place in the vortex plus air fryer oven.
5. Serve and enjoy.

**Nutritional Value (Amount per Serving):**

- Calories 133
- Fat 12.3 g
- Carbohydrates 2.9 g
- Sugar 0.8 g
- Protein 4.3 g
- Cholesterol 46 mg

# Chili Olive Breakfast Casserole

Preparation Time: 10 minutes

Cooking Time: 35 minutes

Serve: 8

**Ingredients:**

- 12 eggs
- 4 oz green chilies, diced
- 2 cups cheddar cheese, grated
- 2 cups cottage cheese, rinsed and drained
- 6 oz olives, pitted and sliced
- 1/4 cup green onions, sliced
- Pepper
- Salt

**Directions:**

1. Add cottage cheese, cheddar cheese, green chilies, green onion, and olives in the greased baking dish.
2. Whisk beaten eggs and pour over cheese mixture. Season with pepper and salt.
3. Select BAKE mode, then set the temperature to 375 F and the time to 35 minutes, then press start.
4. When the display shows Add Food then place the baking dish in the vortex plus air fryer oven.
5. Serve and enjoy.

**Nutritional Value (Amount per Serving):**

- Calories 232
- Fat 13.1 g
- Carbohydrates 14.4 g
- Sugar 6.1 g
- Protein 16.2 g
- Cholesterol 40 mg

# Delicious Breakfast Casserole

Preparation Time: 10 minutes

Cooking Time: 35 minutes

Serve: 4

**Ingredients:**

- 2 eggs
- 4 egg whites
- 2/3 cup parmesan cheese, grated
- 2/3 cup chicken broth
- 1 lb Italian sausage
- 1/4 cup roasted red pepper, sliced
- 1/4 cup pesto sauce
- 1/8 tsp black pepper
- 1/4 tsp sea salt

**Directions:**

1. Brown sausage in a pan over medium heat.
2. Transfer sausage in greased baking dish.
3. Whisk remaining ingredients in a mixing bowl and pour over sausage.
4. Select BAKE mode, then set the temperature to 400 F and the time to 35 minutes, then press start.
5. When the display shows Add Food then place the baking dish in the vortex plus air fryer oven.
6. Serve and enjoy.

**Nutritional Value (Amount per Serving):**

- Calories 558
- Fat 44.3 g
- Carbohydrates 2.8 g
- Sugar 2 g
- Protein 35.6 g
- Cholesterol 191 mg

# Zucchini Breakfast Bread Loaf

Preparation Time: 10 minutes

Cooking Time: 45 minutes

Serve: 12

**Ingredients:**

- 4 eggs
- 1 cup zucchini, shredded and squeeze out all liquid
- 3/4 tsp baking soda
- 1/2 cup coconut flour
- 1 tbsp coconut oil
- 1 banana, mashed
- 1/2 cup walnuts, chopped
- 1 tsp vinegar
- 1/2 tsp nutmeg
- 1 tbsp cinnamon
- 1 tsp liquid stevia
- 1/2 tsp salt

**Directions:**

1. In a large bowl, mix together egg, banana, oil, and stevia.
2. Add all dry ingredients, vinegar, and zucchini and stir until smooth. Add walnuts and stir well.
3. Pour batter into the greased loaf pan.
4. Select BAKE mode, then set the temperature to 350 F and the time to 45 minutes, then press start.
5. When the display shows Add Food then place the loaf pan in the vortex plus air fryer oven.
6. Slice and serve.

**Nutritional Value (Amount per Serving):**

- Calories 78
- Fat 5.8 g
- Carbohydrates 4 g
- Sugar 1.6 g
- Protein 3.4 g
- Cholesterol 55 mg

# Spinach Egg Muffins

Preparation Time: 10 minutes

Cooking Time: 12 minutes

Serve: 6

**Ingredients:**

- 4 eggs
- 6 tbsp cheddar cheese, shredded
- 2 tbsp heavy cream
- 1/4 cup fresh baby spinach, chopped
- 4 bacon slices, cooked chopped
- Pepper
- Salt

**Directions:**

1. Divide spinach and bacon evenly into the 6 silicone muffin molds.
2. In a bowl, whisk eggs with cheddar cheese, heavy cream, pepper, and salt.
3. Pour egg mixture over spinach and bacon.
4. Select BAKE mode, then set the temperature to 380 F and the time to 12 minutes, then press start.
5. When the display shows Add Food then place silicone muffin molds on the cooking tray and place in the vortex plus air fryer oven.
6. Serve and enjoy.

**Nutritional Value (Amount per Serving):**

- Calories 157
- Fat 12.4 g
- Carbohydrates 0.7 g
- Sugar 0.3 g
- Protein 10.3 g
- Cholesterol 137 mg

# Ham Egg Muffins

Preparation Time: 10 minutes

Cooking Time: 18 minutes

Serve: 12

**Ingredients:**

- 6 eggs
- 1 cup cheddar cheese, shredded
- 3/4 cup ham, chopped
- 1/2 tsp baking powder
- 1/4 cup heavy cream
- 1/4 tsp pepper
- 1/2 tsp salt

**Directions:**

1. In a bowl, whisk eggs with baking powder, cream, pepper, and salt. Stir in ham and cheese.
2. Pour egg mixture into the 12 silicone muffin molds.
3. Select BAKE mode, then set the temperature to 380 F and the time to 18 minutes, then press start.
4. When the display shows Add Food then place silicone muffin molds on the cooking tray and place in the vortex plus air fryer oven.
5. Serve and enjoy.

**Nutritional Value (Amount per Serving):**

- Calories 92
- Fat 7 g
- Carbohydrates 0.8 g
- Sugar 0.2 g
- Protein 6.6 g
- Cholesterol 100 mg

# Easy Egg Muffins

Preparation Time: 10 minutes

Cooking Time: 30 minutes

Serve: 12

**Ingredients:**

- 6 eggs
- 1 red bell pepper, chopped
- 1 1/2 tsp dried oregano
- 1/3 cup unsweetened almond milk
- 1 tomato, chopped
- 1/2 cup feta cheese, crumbled
- 1/4 tsp pepper
- 1/8 tsp salt

**Directions:**

1. In a bowl, whisk eggs with milk, oregano, pepper, and salt.
2. Divide cheese, tomato, and bell pepper evenly in 12 silicone muffin molds.
3. Pour egg mixture over cheese vegetable mixture.
4. Select BAKE mode, then set the temperature to 350 F and the time to 25-30 minutes, then press start.
5. When the display shows Add Food then place muffin molds on the cooking tray and place in the vortex plus air fryer oven.
6. Serve and enjoy.

**Nutritional Value (Amount per Serving):**

- Calories 54
- Fat 3.7 g
- Carbohydrates 1.6 g
- Sugar 1.1 g
- Protein 3.9 g
- Cholesterol 87 mg

# Zucchini Gratin

Preparation Time: 10 minutes

Cooking Time: 25 minutes

Serve: 4

**Ingredients:**

- 1 egg, lightly beaten
- 1 1/4 cup unsweetened almond milk
- 3 medium zucchinis, sliced
- 1 tbsp Dijon mustard
- 1/2 cup nutritional yeast
- 1 tsp sea salt

**Directions:**

1. Arrange zucchini slices in the greased baking dish.
2. In a small saucepan, heat milk over low heat and stir in Dijon mustard, nutritional yeast, and sea salt.
3. Add beaten egg and whisk well.
4. Pour sauce over zucchini slices.
5. Select BAKE mode, then set the temperature to 400 F and the time to 25-30 minutes, then press start.
6. When the display shows Add Food then place the baking dish in the vortex plus air fryer oven.
7. Serve and enjoy.

**Nutritional Value (Amount per Serving):**

- Calories 125
- Fat 3.7 g
- Carbohydrates 15 g
- Sugar 2.7 g
- Protein 12.8 g
- Cholesterol 41 mg

# Cheese Egg Bites

Preparation Time: 10 minutes
Cooking Time: 15 minutes
Serve: 4

**Ingredients:**

- 4 eggs
- 1/2 tsp baking powder
- 1/3 cup almond flour
- 1 1/4 cups cheddar cheese, shredded
- 5 bacon slices, cooked & chopped
- 2 oz cream cheese, softened

**Directions:**

1. Add all ingredients into the mixing bowl and mix until well combined and let it sit for 10 minutes.
2. Pour mixture into the silicone muffin pan.
3. Select BAKE mode, then set the temperature to 350 F and the time to 15 minutes, then press start.
4. When the display shows Add Food then place the silicone muffin pan on the cooking tray and place it in the vortex plus air fryer oven.
5. Serve and enjoy.

**Nutritional Value (Amount per Serving):**

- Calories 397
- Fat 32.1 g
- Carbohydrates 2.3 g
- Sugar 0.6 g
- Protein 24.7 g
- Cholesterol 242 mg

# Almond Butter Bread

Preparation Time: 10 minutes

Cooking Time: 45 minutes

Serve: 10

**Ingredients:**

- 3 eggs
- 1/4 cup butter, melted
- 3 1/2 cups almond flour
- 1 cup yogurt
- 1 tsp baking soda
- 1/4 tsp salt

**Directions:**

1. Add all ingredients into the large bowl and mix until well combined.
2. Pour batter into the greased loaf pan.
3. Select BAKE mode, then set the temperature to 350 F and the time to 45 minutes, then press start.
4. When the display shows Add Food then place the loaf pan in the vortex plus air fryer oven.
5. Slice and serve.

**Nutritional Value (Amount per Serving):**

- Calories 301
- Fat 25.8 g
- Carbohydrates 10.2 g
- Sugar 3.2 g
- Protein 11.5 g
- Cholesterol 63 mg

# Cheesy Egg Bites

Preparation Time: 10 minutes

Cooking Time: 20 minutes

Serve: 4

**Ingredients:**

- 3 eggs, lightly beaten
- 1 1/2 cups cheddar cheese
- 1/2 tsp baking powder
- 1/3 cup coconut flour
- 4 oz cream cheese, softened
- 2 cups ham, chopped
- 1/2 tsp garlic powder
- Pepper
- Salt

**Directions:**

1. Add all ingredients into the mixing bowl and mix until well combined then place in the refrigerator for 10-15 minutes.
2. Drop mixture onto the parchment-lined cooking tray using a cookie scoop.
3. Select BAKE mode, then set the temperature to 350 F and the time to 20 minutes, then press start.
4. When the display shows Add Food then place the cooking tray and place in the vortex plus air fryer oven.
5. Serve and enjoy.

**Nutritional Value (Amount per Serving):**

- Calories 434
- Fat 33.2 g
- Carbohydrates 5.4 g
- Sugar 0.7 g
- Protein 28.3 g
- Cholesterol 237 mg

# Breakfast Chicken Egg Cups

Preparation Time: 10 minutes

Cooking Time: 15 minutes

Serve: 12

**Ingredients:**

- 10 eggs
- 1/3 cup green onions, chopped
- 1 cup cooked chicken, chopped
- 1/4 tsp garlic powder
- 1/4 tsp pepper
- 1 tsp sea salt

**Directions:**

1. In a large bowl, whisk eggs with garlic powder, pepper, and salt. Add remaining ingredients and stir well.
2. Pour egg mixture into the 12 silicone muffin molds.
3. Select BAKE mode, then set the temperature to 400 F and the time to 15 minutes, then press start.
4. When the display shows Add Food then place muffin molds on the cooking tray and place in the vortex plus air fryer oven.
5. Serve and enjoy.

**Nutritional Value (Amount per Serving):**

- Calories 71
- Fat 4 g
- Carbohydrates 0.6 g
- Sugar 0.4 g
- Protein 8.1 g
- Cholesterol 145 mg

# Squash Casserole

Preparation Time: 10 minutes

Cooking Time: 25 minutes

Serve: 6

**Ingredients:**

- 12 eggs
- 2 cups spaghetti squash, cooked
- 1 cup cheddar cheese, shredded
- 1 cup heavy cream
- 4 tbsp butter, melted
- 1/2 cup bell pepper, diced
- Pepper
- Salt

**Directions:**

1. In a large bowl, add all ingredients and mix well until combine.
2. Pour mixture into the greased baking dish.
3. Select BAKE mode, then set the temperature to 350 F and the time to 25 minutes, then press start.
4. When the display shows Add Food then place the baking dish in the vortex plus air fryer oven.
5. Serve and enjoy.

**Nutritional Value (Amount per Serving):**

- Calories 352
- Fat 30.3 g
- Carbohydrates 4.6 g
- Sugar 1.3 g
- Protein 16.6 g
- Cholesterol 395 mg

# Chapter 3: Poultry Recipes

## Juicy & Crispy Chicken Drumsticks

Preparation Time: 10 minutes

Cooking Time: 45 minutes

Serve: 6

**Ingredients:**

- 2 lbs chicken drumsticks
- 1 tsp parsley, chopped
- 1 tsp onion powder
- 1 tsp garlic powder
- 1 tsp paprika
- 2 tbsp olive oil
- 1/2 tsp pepper
- 1/2 tsp salt

**Directions:**

1. Add chicken drumsticks and remaining ingredients into the zip-lock bag, seal bag and shake well to coat.
2. Arrange chicken drumsticks onto the cooking tray.
3. Select BAKE mode, then set the temperature to 400 F and the time to 40-45 minutes, then press start.
4. When the display shows Add Food then place the cooking tray in the vortex plus air fryer oven.
5. Serve and enjoy.

**Nutritional Value (Amount per Serving):**

- Calories 300
- Fat 13.4 g
- Carbohydrates 1 g
- Sugar 0.3 g
- Protein 41.8 g
- Cholesterol 133 mg

# Delicious Chicken Casserole

Preparation Time: 10 minutes

Cooking Time: 40 minutes

Serve: 8

**Ingredients:**

- 2 lbs cooked chicken, shredded
- 6 oz cream cheese, softened
- 4 oz butter, melted
- 5 oz ham, cut into small pieces
- 5 oz Swiss cheese slices
- 1 oz fresh lemon juice
- 1 tbsp Dijon mustard
- 1/2 tsp salt

**Directions:**

1. Add chicken in the greased baking dish then top with ham.
2. Add butter, lemon juice, mustard, cream cheese, and salt into the blender and blend until smooth.
3. Pour blended mixture on top of chicken and ham mixture.
4. Arrange Swiss cheese slices on top of sauce.
5. Select BAKE mode, then set the temperature to 350 F and the time to 40 minutes, then press start.
6. When the display shows Add Food then place the baking dish in the vortex plus air fryer oven.
7. Serve and enjoy.

**Nutritional Value (Amount per Serving):**

- Calories 435
- Fat 27.8 g
- Carbohydrates 2.1 g
- Sugar 0.8 g
- Protein 42.7 g
- Cholesterol 164 mg

# Parmesan Chicken Fritters

Preparation Time: 10 minutes

Cooking Time: 10 minutes

Serve: 4

**Ingredients:**

- 1 lb ground chicken
- 1/2 cup parmesan cheese, shredded
- 1/2 tbsp dill, chopped
- 1/2 cup almond flour
- 2 tbsp green onions, chopped
- 1/2 tsp onion powder
- 1/2 tsp garlic powder
- Pepper
- Salt

**Directions:**

1. Add all ingredients into the large bowl and mix until well combined.
2. Make small patties from mixture and place onto the parchment-lined cooking tray.
3. Select AIRFRY mode, then set the temperature to 350 F and the time to 10 minutes, then press start.
4. When the display shows Add Food then place the cooking tray in the vortex plus air fryer oven.
5. Serve and enjoy.

**Nutritional Value (Amount per Serving):**

- Calories 269
- Fat 14.3 g
- Carbohydrates 3.5 g
- Sugar 0.6 g
- Protein 31.7 g
- Cholesterol 87 mg

# Chicken Veggie Fritters

Preparation Time: 10 minutes

Cooking Time: 25 minutes

Serve: 4

**Ingredients:**

- 1 lb ground chicken
- 3/4 cup almond flour
- 1 egg, lightly beaten
- 1 garlic clove, minced
- 1 1/2 cup mozzarella cheese, shredded
- 1/2 cup shallots, chopped
- 2 cups broccoli, chopped
- Pepper
- Salt

**Directions:**

1. Add all ingredients into the large bowl and mix until well combined.
2. Make small patties from mixture and place onto the parchment-lined cooking tray.
3. Select BAKE mode, then set the temperature to 390 F and the time to 25 minutes, then press start.
4. When the display shows Add Food then place the cooking tray in the vortex plus air fryer oven.
5. Turn chicken patties halfway through.
6. Serve and enjoy.

**Nutritional Value (Amount per Serving):**

- Calories 412
- Fat 22.1 g
- Carbohydrates 11.6 g
- Sugar 1.6 g
- Protein 43.5 g
- Cholesterol 147 mg

# Spinach Turkey Meatballs

Preparation Time: 10 minutes

Cooking Time: 25 minutes

Serve: 6

**Ingredients:**

- 1 egg
- 2 lbs ground turkey
- 1/2 tsp garlic, minced
- 1 small onion, minced
- 10 oz frozen spinach, thawed, drained & chopped
- 1/4 tsp pepper
- 1 1/2 tsp salt

**Directions:**

1. Add all ingredients into the bowl and mix until well combined.
2. Make small balls from meat mixture and place onto the parchment-lined cooking tray.
3. Select BAKE mode, then set the temperature to 400 F and the time to 25 minutes, then press start.
4. When the display shows Add Food then place the cooking tray in the vortex plus air fryer oven.
5. Serve and enjoy.

**Nutritional Value (Amount per Serving):**

- Calories 322
- Fat 17.5 g
- Carbohydrates 3 g
- Sugar 0.8 g
- Protein 43.8 g
- Cholesterol 181 mg

# Delicious Turkey Cutlets

Preparation Time: 10 minutes

Cooking Time: 25 minutes

Serve: 4

**Ingredients:**

- 1 egg
- 1 1/2 lbs turkey cutlets
- 1/2 tsp garlic powder
- 1/2 tsp onion powder
- 1/2 tsp dried parsley
- 1/4 cup parmesan cheese, grated
- 1/2 cup almond flour
- Pepper
- Salt

**Directions:**

1. Season turkey cutlets with pepper and salt.
2. Add eggs into the small bowl and whisk well.
3. In a shallow dish, mix together parmesan cheese, garlic powder, onion powder, parsley, and almond flour.
4. Dip each turkey cutlet into the egg then coat with parmesan cheese mixture.
5. Place coated turkey cutlets onto the parchment-lined cooking tray.
6. Select BAKE mode, then set the temperature to 350 F and the time to 25 minutes, then press start.
7. When the display shows Add Food then place the cooking tray in the vortex plus air fryer oven.
8. Turn cutlet halfway through.
9. Serve and enjoy.

**Nutritional Value (Amount per Serving):**

- Calories 405
- Fat 17.8 g
- Carbohydrates 3.8 g
- Sugar 0.8 g
- Protein 56.1 g
- Cholesterol 174 mg

# Flavorful Chicken Skewers

Preparation Time: 10 minutes

Cooking Time: 20 minutes

Serve: 4

**Ingredients:**

* 1 1/2 lbs chicken breast, cut into 1-inch cubes

For marinade:

* 1/4 cup fresh mint leaves
* 4 garlic cloves
* 1/2 cup lemon juice
* 1/4 tsp cayenne
* 1 tbsp vinegar
* 1/2 cup yogurt
* 2 tbsp fresh rosemary, chopped
* 2 tbsp dried oregano
* 1 cup olive oil
* Pepper
* Salt

**Directions:**

1. Add all marinade ingredients into the blender and blend until smooth.
2. Pour blended mixture in a large bowl. Add chicken and coat well and place it in the refrigerator for 1 hour.
3. Slide marinated chicken onto the skewers. Place skewers onto the cooking tray.
4. Select BAKE mode, then set the temperature to 400 F and the time to 15-20 minutes, then press start.
5. When the display shows Add Food then place the cooking tray in the vortex plus air fryer oven.
6. Serve and enjoy.

**Nutritional Value (Amount per Serving):**

* Calories 676
* Fat 55.8 g
* Carbohydrates 6.9 g
* Sugar 3 g
* Protein 38.8 g
* Cholesterol 111 mg

# Herb Chicken Breast

Preparation Time: 10 minutes

Cooking Time: 25 minutes

Serve: 4

**Ingredients:**

- 4 chicken breasts, skinless & boneless
- 1 tbsp olive oil

For rub:

- 1 tsp oregano
- 1 tsp thyme
- 1 tsp parsley
- 1 tsp onion powder
- 1 tsp basil
- Pepper
- Salt

**Directions:**

1. In a small bowl mix together all rub ingredients.
2. Brush chicken with oil and rub with herb mixture.
3. Arrange chicken onto the cooking tray.
4. Select BAKE mode, then set the temperature to 390 F and the time to 25 minutes, then press start.
5. When the display shows Add Food then place the cooking tray in the vortex plus air fryer oven.
6. Turn chicken halfway through.
7. Serve and enjoy.

**Nutritional Value (Amount per Serving):**

- Calories 312
- Fat 14.4 g
- Carbohydrates 0.9 g
- Sugar 0.2 g
- Protein 42.4 g
- Cholesterol 130 mg

# Breaded Chicken Tenders

Preparation Time: 10 minutes

Cooking Time: 20 minutes

Serve: 4

**Ingredients:**

- 3 chicken breasts, cut into strips
- 2 tsp Italian seasoning
- 1/2 cup pork rinds, crushed
- 1/2 cup parmesan cheese, grated
- 1/2 cup mayonnaise

**Directions:**

1. In a small bowl, add mayonnaise.
2. In a shallow dish, mix together pork rinds, parmesan cheese, and Italian seasoning.
3. Dip the chicken strip into the mayonnaise then coats with pork rind mixture.
4. Place coated chicken strips onto the parchment-lined cooking tray.
5. Select BAKE mode, then set the temperature to 350 F and the time to 20 minutes, then press start.
6. When the display shows Add Food then place the cooking tray in the vortex plus air fryer oven.
7. Serve and enjoy.

**Nutritional Value (Amount per Serving):**

- Calories 376
- Fat 21.7 g
- Carbohydrates 7.7 g
- Sugar 2.1 g
- Protein 36.7 g
- Cholesterol 117 mg

# Feta Turkey Patties

Preparation Time: 10 minutes

Cooking Time: 22 minutes

Serve: 4

**Ingredients:**

- 1 lb ground turkey
- 4 oz feta cheese, crumbled
- 1 1/4 cup spinach, chopped
- 1 tsp Italian seasoning
- 1 tbsp olive oil
- 1 tbsp garlic paste
- Pepper
- Salt

**Directions:**

1. Add all ingredients into the bowl and mix until well combined.
2. Make four equal shapes of patties from the mixture and place them onto the cooking tray.
3. Select AIRFRY mode, then set the temperature to 390 F and the time to 22 minutes, then press start.
4. When the display shows Add Food then place the cooking tray in the vortex plus air fryer oven.
5. Turn chicken patties through.
6. Serve and enjoy.

**Nutritional Value (Amount per Serving):**

- Calories 335
- Fat 22.4 g
- Carbohydrates 2.3 g
- Sugar 1.3 g
- Protein 35.5 g
- Cholesterol 142 mg

# Baked Parmesan Chicken Breasts

Preparation Time: 10 minutes

Cooking Time: 45 minutes

Serve: 4

**Ingredients:**

- 4 chicken breasts, skinless & boneless
- 5 Plain Greek yogurts
- 1 tsp garlic powder
- 1/2 cup parmesan cheese, grated
- 1/2 tsp pepper
- 1 tsp salt

**Directions:**

1. Season chicken breasts with pepper and salt and place into the baking dish.
2. Mix together yogurt, garlic powder, and parmesan cheese and pour over chicken breasts. Cover dish with foil.
3. Select BAKE mode, then set the temperature to 375 F and the time to 45 minutes, then press start.
4. When the display shows Add Food then place the baking dish in the vortex plus air fryer oven.
5. Serve and enjoy.

**Nutritional Value (Amount per Serving):**

- Calories 347
- Fat 13.3 g
- Carbohydrates 5.1 g
- Sugar 3.9 g
- Protein 49.3 g
- Cholesterol 139 mg

# Tasty Chicken Nuggets

Preparation Time: 10 minutes

Cooking Time: 25 minutes

Serve: 4

**Ingredients:**

- 1 1/2 lbs chicken breast, boneless & cut into chunks
- 1/4 cup parmesan cheese, shredded
- 1/4 cup mayonnaise
- 1/2 tsp garlic powder
- 1/4 tsp salt

**Directions:**

1. In a bowl, mix together mayonnaise, garlic powder, cheese, and salt. Add chicken chunks and toss until well coated.
2. Arrange chicken chunks onto the parchment-lined cooking tray.
3. Select BAKE mode, then set the temperature to 400 F and the time to 25 minutes, then press start.
4. When the display shows Add Food then place the cooking tray in the vortex plus air fryer oven.
5. Serve and enjoy.

**Nutritional Value (Amount per Serving):**

- Calories 270
- Fat 10.4 g
- Carbohydrates 4 g
- Sugar 1 g
- Protein 38.1 g
- Cholesterol 117 mg

# BBQ Chicken Wings

Preparation Time: 10 minutes

Cooking Time: 45 minutes

Serve: 4

**Ingredients:**

- 1 1/2 lbs chicken wings
- 1/4 cup BBQ spice rub
- 1 tbsp olive oil

**Directions:**

1. Brush chicken wings with oil and season with BBQ spice rub and place onto the cooking tray.
2. Select BAKE mode, then set the temperature to 390 F and the time to 45 minutes, then press start.
3. When the display shows Add Food then place the cooking tray in the vortex plus air fryer oven.
4. Serve and enjoy.

**Nutritional Value (Amount per Serving):**

- Calories 386
- Fat 18 g
- Carbohydrates 4.2 g
- Sugar 0.5 g
- Protein 49.7 g
- Cholesterol 151 mg

# Tasty Jerk Chicken Wings

Preparation Time: 10 minutes

Cooking Time: 20 minutes

Serve: 2

**Ingredients:**

- 1 lb chicken wings
- 1 tsp olive oil
- 1 tbsp arrowroot
- 1 tbsp jerk seasoning
- Pepper
- Salt

**Directions:**

1. Add chicken wings and remaining ingredients into the mixing bowl and toss well.
2. Arrange chicken wings onto the cooking tray.
3. Select AIRFRY mode, then set the temperature to 380 F and the time to 20 minutes, then press start.
4. When the display shows Add Food then place the cooking tray in the vortex plus air fryer oven.
5. Turn chicken wings halfway through.
6. Serve and enjoy.

**Nutritional Value (Amount per Serving):**

- Calories 453
- Fat 19.2 g
- Carbohydrates 0.5 g
- Sugar 0 g
- Protein 65.8 g
- Cholesterol 202 mg

# Healthy Chicken Patties

Preparation Time: 10 minutes

Cooking Time: 25 minutes

Serve: 4

**Ingredients:**

- 1 lb ground chicken
- 1 egg, lightly beaten
- 1 cup Monterey jack cheese, grated
- 1 cup carrot, grated
- 1 cup cauliflower, grated
- 1/8 tsp red pepper flakes
- 2 garlic cloves, minced
- 1/2 cup onion, minced
- 3/4 cup almond flour
- Pepper
- Salt

**Directions:**

1. Add all ingredients into the large bowl and mix until well combined.
2. Make small patties from mixture and place onto the parchment-lined cooking tray.
3. Select BAKE mode, then set the temperature to 400 F and the time to 25 minutes, then press start.
4. When the display shows Add Food then place the cooking tray in the vortex plus air fryer oven.
5. Serve and enjoy.

**Nutritional Value (Amount per Serving):**

- Calories 482
- Fat 28.6 g
- Carbohydrates 10.7 g
- Sugar 3.6 g
- Protein 46.6 g
- Cholesterol 167 mg

# Chapter 4: Meat Recipes

## Air Fryer Pork Ribs

Preparation Time: 10 minutes

Cooking Time: 20 minutes

Serve: 2

**Ingredients:**

- 1 1/2 lbs pork ribs
- 2 1/2 tbsp olive oil
- 1 1/2 tbsp paprika
- 1 tbsp salt

**Directions:**

1. Brush pork ribs with oil and season with paprika and salt.
2. Place pork ribs onto the cooking tray.
3. Select AIRFRY mode, then set the temperature to 350 F and the time to 20 minutes, then press start.
4. When the display shows Add Food then place the cooking tray in the vortex plus air fryer oven.
5. Serve and enjoy.

**Nutritional Value (Amount per Serving):**

- Calories 1094
- Fat 78.4 g
- Carbohydrates 2.9 g
- Sugar 0.5 g
- Protein 90.9 g
- Cholesterol 350 mg

# Jamaican Pork Butt

Preparation Time: 10 minutes
Cooking Time: 20 minutes
Serve: 4

**Ingredients:**

- 1 1/2 lbs pork butt, chopped into pieces
- 1/4 cup jerk paste
- Pepper
- Salt

**Directions:**

1. Add meat and jerk paste into the bowl and mix well, cover and place in refrigerator overnight.
2. Place marinated meat onto the cooking tray.
3. Select AIRFRY mode, then set the temperature to 390 F and the time to 20 minutes, then press start.
4. When the display shows Add Food then place the cooking tray in the vortex plus air fryer oven.
5. Serve and enjoy.

**Nutritional Value (Amount per Serving):**

- Calories 348
- Fat 12.8 g
- Carbohydrates 1.4 g
- Sugar 1 g
- Protein 53.1 g
- Cholesterol 156 mg

# Meatballs

Preparation Time: 10 minutes

Cooking Time: 20 minutes

Serve: 8

**Ingredients:**

- 2 lbs ground beef
- 1 cup almond flour
- 1/2 cup coconut flour
- 12 oz jar roasted red peppers
- 2 eggs, lightly beaten
- 1/4 cup fresh parsley, chopped
- 1/2 cup fresh basil, chopped
- 1/3 cup tomato sauce
- 1/4 tsp pepper
- 1/2 tsp salt

**Directions:**

1. Add all ingredients into the large bowl and mix until well combined.
2. Make small meatballs from mixture and place onto the cooking tray.
3. Select BAKE mode, then set the temperature to 350 F and the time to 20 minutes, then press start.
4. When the display shows Add Food then place the cooking tray in the vortex plus air fryer oven.
5. Serve and enjoy.

**Nutritional Value (Amount per Serving):**

- Calories 367
- Fat 15.3 g
- Carbohydrates 11.9 g
- Sugar 1.1 g
- Protein 40.7 g
- Cholesterol 142 mg

# Juicy & Tender Pork Chops

Preparation Time: 10 minutes

Cooking Time: 15 minutes

Serve: 4

**Ingredients:**

- 4 pork chops, boneless
- 1 tsp onion powder
- 1 tsp smoked paprika
- 4 tbsp olive oil
- Pepper
- Salt

**Directions:**

1. Brush pork chops with oil and season with onion powder, paprika, pepper, and salt.
2. Place pork chops onto the cooking tray.
3. Select BAKE mode, then set the temperature to 400 F and the time to 15 minutes, then press start.
4. When the display shows Add Food then place the cooking tray in the vortex plus air fryer oven.
5. Serve and enjoy.

**Nutritional Value (Amount per Serving):**

- Calories 380
- Fat 34 g
- Carbohydrates 0.8 g
- Sugar 0.3 g
- Protein 18.1 g
- Cholesterol 69 mg

# Tasty Stuffed Peppers

Preparation Time: 10 minutes

Cooking Time: 8 minutes

Serve: 12

**Ingredients:**

- 6 jalapeno peppers, cut in half & remove seeds
- 1 1/2 tbsp taco seasoning
- 1/2 lb ground pork
- 1/4 cup mozzarella cheese, shredded

**Directions:**

1. Browned the meat in a pan. Remove pan from heat.
2. Add taco seasoning and mix well.
3. Stuff meat into each jalapeno half.
4. Place stuffed jalapeno peppers onto the cooking tray and top with cheese.
5. Select AIRFRY mode, then set the temperature to 320 F and the time to 8 minutes, then press start.
6. When the display shows Add Food then place the cooking tray in the vortex plus air fryer oven.
7. Serve and enjoy.

**Nutritional Value (Amount per Serving):**

- Calories 34
- Fat 1 g
- Carbohydrates 0.7 g
- Sugar 0.2 g
- Protein 5.4 g
- Cholesterol 15 mg

# Pecan Crust Pork Chops

Preparation Time: 10 minutes

Cooking Time: 12 minutes

Serve: 6

**Ingredients:**

- 1 egg
- 6 pork chops, boneless
- 1 tsp garlic, crushed
- 1 tbsp water
- 1 tsp Dijon mustard
- 1 tsp garlic powder
- 1 tsp onion powder
- 2 tsp Italian seasoning
- 1/3 cup arrowroot
- 1 cup pecan pieces, crushed
- 1/4 tsp sea salt

**Directions:**

1. In a small bowl, whisk eggs with garlic, water, and Dijon mustard.
2. In a shallow dish, mix together pecans, garlic powder, onion powder, Italian seasoning, arrowroot, and sea salt.
3. Dip pork chop in egg mixture then coats with pecan mixture.
4. Place coated pork chops onto the cooking tray.
5. Select AIRFRY mode, then set the temperature to 400 F and the time to 12 minutes, then press start.
6. When the display shows Add Food then place the cooking tray in the vortex plus air fryer oven.
7. Flip pork chops halfway through.
8. Serve and enjoy.

**Nutritional Value (Amount per Serving):**

- Calories 296
- Fat 22.8 g
- Carbohydrates 2.3 g
- Sugar 0.5 g
- Protein 19.6 g
- Cholesterol 97 mg

# Baked Beef with Broccoli

Preparation Time: 10 minutes

Cooking Time: 25 minutes

Serve: 2

**Ingredients:**

- 1/2 lb beef stew meat, cut into pieces
- 1 tbsp vinegar
- 1 garlic clove, minced
- 1 tbsp olive oil
- 1/2 cup broccoli florets
- 1 onion, sliced
- Pepper
- Salt

**Directions:**

1. Add meat and remaining ingredients into the large bowl and toss well and spread onto the cooking tray.
2. Select BAKE mode, then set the temperature to 390 F and the time to 25 minutes, then press start.
3. When the display shows Add Food then place the cooking tray in the vortex plus air fryer oven.
4. Serve and enjoy.

**Nutritional Value (Amount per Serving):**

- Calories 304
- Fat 14.2 g
- Carbohydrates 7.3 g
- Sugar 2.8 g
- Protein 35.8 g
- Cholesterol 101 mg

# Simple Herbed Beef Tips

Preparation Time: 10 minutes

Cooking Time: 20 minutes

Serve: 6

**Ingredients:**

- 2 lbs sirloin steak, cut into 1-inch cubes
- 1/4 tsp red chili flakes
- 1/2 tsp black pepper
- 1/2 tsp dried thyme
- 1 tsp onion powder
- 1 tsp dried oregano
- 2 tbsp lemon juice
- 2 tbsp water
- 1/4 cup olive oil
- 1 cup fresh parsley, chopped
- 2 garlic cloves, minced
- 1/2 tsp salt

**Directions:**

1. Add meat cubes and remaining ingredients into the zip-lock bag, seal bag, and place in the refrigerator overnight.
2. Place marinated meat cubes onto the parchment-lined cooking tray.
3. Select BAKE mode, then set the temperature to 400 F and the time to 20 minutes, then press start.
4. When the display shows Add Food then place the cooking tray in the vortex plus air fryer oven.
5. Serve and enjoy.

**Nutritional Value (Amount per Serving):**

- Calories 362
- Fat 18 g
- Carbohydrates 1.7 g
- Sugar 0.4 g
- Protein 46.4 g
- Cholesterol 135 mg

# Burger Patties

Preparation Time: 10 minutes

Cooking Time: 15 minutes

Serve: 6

**Ingredients:**

- 2 lbs ground beef
- 1 tsp garlic powder
- 1 cup mozzarella cheese, grated
- 1 tsp onion powder
- Pepper
- Salt

**Directions:**

1. Add all ingredients into the large bowl and mix until well combined.
2. Make small patties from meat mixture and place onto the parchment-lined cooking tray.
3. Select BAKE mode, then set the temperature to 400 F and the time to 15 minutes, then press start.
4. When the display shows Add Food then place the cooking tray in the vortex plus air fryer oven.
5. Serve and enjoy.

**Nutritional Value (Amount per Serving):**

- Calories 297
- Fat 10.3 g
- Carbohydrates 0.8 g
- Sugar 0.3 g
- Protein 47.3 g
- Cholesterol 138 mg

# Delicious Kebab

Preparation Time: 10 minutes

Cooking Time: 10 minutes

Serve: 4

**Ingredients:**

- 1/2 lb ground beef
- 1/2 lb ground pork
- 2 tbsp kabab spice mix
- 1 tbsp garlic, minced
- 1/4 cup fresh parsley, chopped
- 1 tbsp olive oil
- 1 tsp salt

**Directions:**

1. Add all ingredients into the bowl and mix until well combined. Cover and place in the refrigerator for 30 minutes.
2. Divide the mixture evenly in 4 portions and make sausage shape kabab.
3. Place kababs onto the cooking tray.
4. Select AIRFRY mode, then set the temperature to 370 F and the time to 10 minutes, then press start.
5. When the display shows Add Food then place the cooking tray in the vortex plus air fryer oven.
6. Serve and enjoy.

**Nutritional Value (Amount per Serving):**

- Calories 231
- Fat 9.3 g
- Carbohydrates 2 g
- Sugar 0.2 g
- Protein 32.8 g
- Cholesterol 92 mg

# Flavorful Bone-in Pork Chops

Preparation Time: 10 minutes

Cooking Time: 20 minutes

Serve: 3

**Ingredients:**

- 1 1/2 lb pork chops, bone-in
- 1 tsp paprika
- 1/2 tsp onion powder
- 1/2 tsp pepper
- 4 tbsp olive oil
- 1 tsp salt

**Directions:**

1. In a small bowl, mix together paprika, onion powder, pepper, and salt.
2. Brush pork chops with oil and rub with spice mixture.
3. Place pork chops onto the cooking tray.
4. Select BAKE mode, then set the temperature to 400 F and the time to 15-20 minutes, then press start.
5. When the display shows Add Food then place the cooking tray in the vortex plus air fryer oven.
6. Serve and enjoy.

**Nutritional Value (Amount per Serving):**

- Calories 890
- Fat 75.1 g
- Carbohydrates 0.9 g
- Sugar 0.2 g
- Protein 51.1 g
- Cholesterol 195 mg

# Creole Cheese Pork Chops

Preparation Time: 10 minutes

Cooking Time: 12 minutes

Serve: 6

**Ingredients:**

- 1 1/2 lbs pork chops, boneless
- 1 tsp Creole seasoning
- 1/4 cup mozzarella cheese, grated
- 1/3 cup almond flour
- 1 tsp paprika
- 1 tsp garlic powder

**Directions:**

1. Add pork chops and remaining ingredients into the zip-lock bag, seal bag shakes well.
2. Place coated pork chops onto the parchment-lined cooking tray.
3. Select AIRFRY mode, then set the temperature to 360 F and the time to 12 minutes, then press start.
4. When the display shows Add Food then place the cooking tray in the vortex plus air fryer oven.
5. Serve and enjoy.

**Nutritional Value (Amount per Serving):**

- Calories 404
- Fat 31.6 g
- Carbohydrates 1.9 g
- Sugar 0.4 g
- Protein 27.3 g
- Cholesterol 98 mg

# Delicious Beef Satay

Preparation Time: 10 minutes

Cooking Time: 8 minutes

Serve: 2

**Ingredients:**

- 1 lb beef flank steak, sliced into long strips
- 1 tbsp fish sauce
- 2 tbsp olive oil
- 1 tsp hot sauce
- 1 tbsp Swerve
- 1 tbsp garlic, minced
- 1 tbsp ginger, minced
- 1 tbsp soy sauce
- 1/2 cup cilantro, chopped
- 1 tsp ground coriander

**Directions:**

1. Add all ingredients into the zip-lock bag, seal bag, and shake well. Place into the refrigerator for 1 hour.
2. Place marinated meat onto the cooking tray.
3. Select AIRFRY mode, then set the temperature to 400 F and the time to 8 minutes, then press start.
4. When the display shows Add Food then place the cooking tray in the vortex plus air fryer oven.
5. Serve and enjoy.

**Nutritional Value (Amount per Serving):**

- Calories 568
- Fat 28.3 g
- Carbohydrates 5.4 g
- Sugar 0.7 g
- Protein 70.4 g
- Cholesterol 203 mg

# Delicious Blackend Pork Tenderloin

Preparation Time: 10 minutes

Cooking Time: 12 minutes

Serve: 6

**Ingredients:**

- 1 1/2 lbs pork tenderloin
- 1/2 cup Worcestershire sauce
- 2/3 cup olive oil
- 1/2 tsp black pepper
- 1 tsp ground red pepper
- 1 tbsp dried tarragon
- 1 tbsp paprika
- 1 tbsp dried oregano
- 1 tbsp dried thyme
- 1 tbsp onion powder
- 1 tbsp garlic powder
- 1 tsp salt

**Directions:**

1. Add pork tenderloin and remaining ingredients into the large zip-lock bag, seal bag, and place in the refrigerator overnight.
2. Remove pork tenderloin from marinade and place onto the parchment-lined cooking tray.
3. Select BAKE mode, then set the temperature to 400 F and the time to 10-12 minutes, then press start.
4. When the display shows Add Food then place the cooking tray in the vortex plus air fryer oven.
5. Slice and serve.

**Nutritional Value (Amount per Serving):**

- Calories 392
- Fat 26.7 g
- Carbohydrates 7.8 g
- Sugar 4.9 g
- Protein 30.5 g
- Cholesterol 83 mg

# Stuffed Pork Chops

Preparation Time: 10 minutes

Cooking Time: 35 minutes

Serve: 4

**Ingredients:**

- 4 pork chops, boneless and thick-cut
- 2 tbsp olives, chopped
- 1 tbsp garlic, minced
- 2 tbsp fresh parsley, chopped
- 2 tbsp sun-dried tomatoes, chopped
- 1/2 cup goat cheese, crumbled

**Directions:**

1. In a bowl, combine together feta cheese, garlic, parsley, olives, and sun-dried tomatoes.
2. Stuff cheese mixture into each pork chops and place pork chops onto the cooking tray.
3. Select BAKE mode, then set the temperature to 375 F and the time to 35 minutes, then press start.
4. When the display shows Add Food then place the cooking tray in the vortex plus air fryer oven.
5. Serve and enjoy.

**Nutritional Value (Amount per Serving):**

- Calories 317
- Fat 24.7 g
- Carbohydrates 1.5 g
- Sugar 0.4 g
- Protein 21.7 g
- Cholesterol 81 mg

# Chapter 5: Vegetable Recipes

## Buffalo Cauliflower

Preparation Time: 10 minutes

Cooking Time: 8 minutes

Serve: 4

**Ingredients:**

- 12 oz cauliflower florets
- 1/4 tsp pepper
- 3 tbsp hot sauce
- 1/2 tsp salt

**Directions:**

1. Add all ingredients to the bowl and toss well.
2. Add cauliflower mixture into the baking dish.
3. Select BAKE mode, then set the temperature to 400 F and the time to 8 minutes, then press start.
4. When the display shows Add Food then place the baking dish in the vortex plus air fryer oven.
5. Serve and enjoy.

**Nutritional Value (Amount per Serving):**

- Calories 23
- Fat 0.1 g
- Carbohydrates 4.8 g
- Sugar 2.2 g
- Protein 1.8 g
- Cholesterol 0 mg

# Cauliflower Rice

Preparation Time: 10 minutes

Cooking Time: 15 minutes

Serve: 3

**Ingredients:**

- 1 cauliflower head, cut into florets
- 2 chilies, chopped
- 2 garlic cloves, chopped
- 1 tomato, chopped
- 1 onion, chopped
- 2 tbsp olive oil
- 1 tsp white pepper
- 1 tsp black pepper
- 1 tbsp dried thyme
- 2 tbsp tomato paste
- 1/2 tsp salt

**Directions:**

1. Add cauliflower florets into the food processor and process until it looks like rice.
2. Stir in tomato paste, tomatoes, and spices and mix well.
3. Spread cauliflower mixture in a baking dish and drizzle with olive oil.
4. Select BAKE mode, then set the temperature to 400 F and the time to 15 minutes, then press start.
5. When the display shows Add Food then place the baking dish in the vortex plus air fryer oven.
6. Serve and enjoy.

**Nutritional Value (Amount per Serving):**

- Calories 138
- Fat 9.7 g
- Carbohydrates 12.8 g
- Sugar 5.7 g
- Protein 3.1 g
- Cholesterol 0 mg

# Perfect Roasted Brussels Sprouts

Preparation Time: 10 minutes

Cooking Time: 25 minutes

Serve: 4

**Ingredients:**

- 15 oz Brussels sprouts
- 1/4 cup almond flour
- 1/4 cup parmesan cheese, grated
- 1 tbsp garlic, minced
- 1/4 tsp pepper
- 3 tbsp olive oil
- 1/2 tsp kosher salt

**Directions:**

1. Add Brussels sprouts and remaining ingredients into the mixing bowl and toss well.
2. Transfer brussels sprout mixture onto the parchment-lined cooking tray.
3. Select BAKE mode, then set the temperature to 400 F and the time to 25 minutes, then press start.
4. When the display shows Add Food then place the cooking tray in the vortex plus air fryer oven.
5. Serve and enjoy.

**Nutritional Value (Amount per Serving):**

- Calories 190
- Fat 15.8 g
- Carbohydrates 10 g
- Sugar 2.1 g
- Protein 6.2 g
- Cholesterol 4 mg

# Baked Parmesan Fennel

Preparation Time: 10 minutes

Cooking Time: 35 minutes

Serve: 6

**Ingredients:**

- 3 fennel bulbs, trimmed & split lengthwise
- 4 sprigs thyme
- 1/3 cup parmesan cheese, grated
- 1 tbsp butter, softened
- Pepper
- Salt

**Directions:**

1. Boil fennel bulbs for 15 minutes or until tender. Drain fennel and pat dry with a paper towel.
2. Place fennel cut side up in the baking dish. Top with butter, cheese, thyme, pepper, and salt.
3. Select BAKE mode, then set the temperature to 400 F and the time to 20 minutes, then press start.
4. When the display shows Add Food then place the baking dish in the vortex plus air fryer oven.
5. Serve and enjoy.

**Nutritional Value (Amount per Serving):**

- Calories 75
- Fat 3.4 g
- Carbohydrates 10 g
- Sugar 0 g
- Protein 3.3 g
- Cholesterol 9 mg

# Tasty Baked Cabbage

Preparation Time: 10 minutes

Cooking Time: 25 minutes

Serve: 2

**Ingredients:**

- 2 lbs medium cabbage, thin shreds
- 3 tbsp butter, melted
- 1 tbsp paprika
- 1 tbsp garlic powder
- 1 tsp salt

**Directions:**

1. Add cabbage, butter, paprika, garlic powder, and salt into the mixing bowl and toss well.
2. Add cabbage mixture into the baking dish.
3. Select BAKE mode, then set the temperature to 400 F and the time to 25 minutes, then press start.
4. When the display shows Add Food then place the baking dish in the vortex plus air fryer oven.
5. Serve and enjoy.

**Nutritional Value (Amount per Serving):**

- Calories 224
- Fat 17.8 g
- Carbohydrates 11.8 g
- Sugar 1.4 g
- Protein 3.7 g
- Cholesterol 46 mg

# Feta Cheese Stuffed Peppers

Preparation Time: 10 minutes

Cooking Time: 50 minutes

Serve: 4

**Ingredients:**

- 4 eggs
- 1/4 cup feta cheese, crumbled
- 1/2 cup broccoli, cooked
- 2 bell peppers, cut in half and remove seeds
- 1/2 cup cheddar cheese, grated
- 1/2 tsp garlic powder
- 1 tsp dried thyme
- 1/4 tsp pepper
- 1/2 tsp salt

**Directions:**

1. Place bell peppers half in a baking dish. Cut side up.
2. Stuff feta and broccoli into the peppers.
3. Beat egg in a bowl with seasoning and pour egg mixture into the pepper over feta and broccoli.
4. Select BAKE mode, then set the temperature to 350 F and the time to 45-50 minutes, then press start.
5. When the display shows Add Food then place the baking dish in the vortex plus air fryer oven.
6. Add grated cheese on top and BAKE for 10 minutes more or until cheese melted.
7. Serve and enjoy.

**Nutritional Value (Amount per Serving):**

- Calories 170
- Fat 11.3 g
- Carbohydrates 6.7 g
- Sugar 4.1 g
- Protein 11.4 g
- Cholesterol 187 mg

# Lemon Garlic Roasted Eggplant

Preparation Time: 10 minutes

Cooking Time: 20 minutes

Serve: 6

**Ingredients:**

- 2 eggplants remove stems and cut into 1-inch pieces
- 1 tsp garlic powder
- 1 tsp onion powder
- 1 tbsp olive oil
- 1 tbsp lemon juice
- Pepper
- Salt

**Directions:**

1. Add all ingredients except lemon juice into the bowl and toss well.
2. Place eggplant mixture into the baking dish.
3. Select BAKE mode, then set the temperature to 320 F and the time to 20 minutes, then press start.
4. When the display shows Add Food then place the baking dish in the vortex plus air fryer oven.
5. Stir eggplant mixture after 15 minutes.
6. Serve and enjoy.

**Nutritional Value (Amount per Serving):**

- Calories 24
- Fat 3.5 g
- Carbohydrates 3.7 g
- Sugar 1 g
- Protein 0.5 g
- Cholesterol 0 mg

# Eggplant Zucchini Casserole

Preparation Time: 10 minutes

Cooking Time: 35 minutes

Serve: 6

**Ingredients:**

- 3 zucchinis, sliced
- 1 cup cherry tomatoes, halved
- 1 medium eggplant, sliced
- 1 tbsp olive oil
- 3 garlic cloves, minced
- 4 tbsp basil, chopped
- 3 oz parmesan cheese, grated
- 1/4 cup parsley, chopped
- 1/4 tsp pepper
- 1/4 tsp salt

**Directions:**

1. Add all ingredients into the large bowl and toss well to combine.
2. Pour eggplant mixture into a greased baking dish.
3. Select BAKE mode, then set the temperature to 350 F and the time to 35 minutes, then press start.
4. When the display shows Add Food then place the baking dish in the vortex plus air fryer oven.
5. Serve and enjoy.

**Nutritional Value (Amount per Serving):**

- Calories 109
- Fat 5.8 g
- Carbohydrates 10.2 g
- Sugar 4.8 g
- Protein 7 g
- Cholesterol 10 mg

# Basil Pesto Spaghetti Squash

Preparation Time: 10 minutes

Cooking Time: 10 minutes

Serve: 4

**Ingredients:**

- 2 cups spaghetti squash, cooked and drained
- 4 oz mozzarella cheese, cubed
- 1/4 cup basil pesto
- 1/2 cup ricotta cheese
- 1 tbsp olive oil
- Pepper
- Salt

**Directions:**

1. In a bowl, combine together olive oil and squash. Season with pepper and salt.
2. Spread squash mixture in greased baking dish.
3. Spread mozzarella cheese and ricotta cheese on top.
4. Select BAKE mode, then set the temperature to 375 F and the time to 10 minutes, then press start.
5. When the display shows Add Food then place the baking dish in the vortex plus air fryer oven.
6. Drizzle with basil pesto and serve.

**Nutritional Value (Amount per Serving):**

- Calories 169
- Fat 11.3 g
- Carbohydrates 6.1 g
- Sugar 0.1 g
- Protein 11.9 g
- Cholesterol 25 mg

# Parmesan Green Bean Casserole

Preparation Time: 10 minutes

Cooking Time: 20 minutes

Serve: 4

**Ingredients:**

- 1 lb green beans, trimmed and cut into pieces
- 1/4 cup olive oil
- 2 oz pecans, crushed
- 1 small onion, chopped
- 2 tbsp lemon zest
- 1/4 cup parmesan cheese, shredded

**Directions:**

1. Add all ingredients into the mixing bowl and toss well.
2. Spread green bean mixture into the baking dish.
3. Select BAKE mode, then set the temperature to 400 F and the time to 20 minutes, then press start.
4. When the display shows Add Food then place the baking dish in the vortex plus air fryer oven.
5. Serve and enjoy.

**Nutritional Value (Amount per Serving):**

- Calories 269
- Fat 24.1 g
- Carbohydrates 12.6 g
- Sugar 3 g
- Protein 5.7 g
- Cholesterol 4 mg

# Baked Cherry Tomatoes & Zucchini

Preparation Time: 10 minutes

Cooking Time: 35 minutes

Serve: 6

**Ingredients:**

- 2 1/2 lbs zucchini, cut into quarters
- 6 garlic cloves, crushed
- 10 oz cherry tomatoes cut in half
- 1/3 cup parsley, chopped
- 1 tsp dried basil
- 1/2 cup parmesan cheese, shredded
- 1/2 tsp black pepper
- 3/4 tsp salt

**Directions:**

1. Add all ingredients except parsley into the large mixing bowl and stir well to combine.
2. Pour egg mixture into the greased baking dish.
3. Select BAKE mode, then set the temperature to 350 F and the time to 35 minutes, then press start.
4. When the display shows Add Food then place the baking dish in the vortex plus air fryer oven.
5. Garnish with parsley and serve.

**Nutritional Value (Amount per Serving):**

- Calories 69
- Fat 2.1 g
- Carbohydrates 9.8 g
- Sugar 4.6 g
- Protein 5.4 g
- Cholesterol 5 mg

# Simple Roasted Beets

Preparation Time: 10 minutes

Cooking Time: 40 minutes

Serve: 4

**Ingredients:**

- 3 large beets, 1 1/2-inch chunk
- 1 tsp orange zest
- 1/2 tsp pepper
- 1 tsp thyme, minced
- 1 tbsp olive oil
- 1 tsp kosher salt

**Directions:**

1. In a large bowl, toss beets with remaining ingredients.
2. Spread beets onto the cooking tray.
3. Select BAKE mode, then set the temperature to 400 F and the time to 35-40 minutes, then press start.
4. When the display shows Add Food then place the cooking tray in the vortex plus air fryer oven.
5. Serve and enjoy.

**Nutritional Value (Amount per Serving):**

- Calories 65
- Fat 3.7 g
- Carbohydrates 7.9 g
- Sugar 6 g
- Protein 1.3 g
- Cholesterol 0 mg

# Thyme Tomatoes

Preparation Time: 10 minutes

Cooking Time: 15 minutes

Serve: 4

**Ingredients:**

- 4 tomatoes cut in half
- 1/2 tsp dried thyme
- 1 garlic clove, minced
- 1 tbsp olive oil
- Pepper
- Salt

**Directions:**

1. Toss tomatoes with olive oil, garlic, pepper, salt, and thyme.
2. Place the tomatoes cut side up in a baking dish.
3. Select BAKE mode, then set the temperature to 390 F and the time to 15 minutes, then press start.
4. When the display shows Add Food then place the baking dish in the vortex plus air fryer oven.
5. Serve and enjoy.

**Nutritional Value (Amount per Serving):**

- Calories 54
- Fat 3.8 g
- Carbohydrates 5.1 g
- Sugar 3.2 g
- Protein 1.1 g
- Cholesterol 0 mg

# Chili Herb Tomatoes

Preparation Time: 10 minutes

Cooking Time: 8 minutes

Serve: 4

**Ingredients:**

- 2 large tomatoes, cut into 4 slices
- 1 tbsp oregano, dried
- 1/4 tsp black pepper
- 1/4 cup balsamic vinegar
- 1 tsp red pepper flakes
- 1/2 tsp sea salt

**Directions:**

1. Add vinegar, salt, oregano, red pepper flakes, and pepper into the bowl and stir well.
2. Dip each tomato slice into the vinegar mixture and place it in a baking dish.
3. Select AIRFRY mode, then set the temperature to 360 F and the time to 5-8 minutes, then press start.
4. When the display shows Add Food then place the baking dish in the vortex plus air fryer oven.
5. Serve and enjoy.

**Nutritional Value (Amount per Serving):**

- Calories 25
- Fat 0.4 g
- Carbohydrates 4.7 g
- Sugar 2.6 g
- Protein 1 g
- Cholesterol 0 mg

# Lemon Parmesan Broccoli

Preparation Time: 10 minutes

Cooking Time: 25 minutes

Serve: 2

**Ingredients:**

- 4 cups broccoli florets
- 4 garlic cloves, sliced
- 3 tbsp coconut oil
- 1 lemon juice
- 1 cup parmesan cheese, grated
- 1/2 tsp pepper
- 1 1/2 tsp salt

**Directions:**

1. In a bowl, toss broccoli florets with coconut oil. Add garlic and season with pepper and salt.
2. Spread broccoli in baking dish.
3. Select BAKE mode, then set the temperature to 400 F and the time to 20 minutes, then press start.
4. When the display shows Add Food then place the baking dish in the vortex plus air fryer oven.
5. Sprinkle with half parmesan cheese and BAKE for 5 minutes more.
6. Add remaining parmesan cheese and lemon juice. Stir well and serve.

**Nutritional Value (Amount per Serving):**

- Calories 356
- Fat 30.3 g
- Carbohydrates 8.4 g
- Sugar 1.6 g
- Protein 17.1 g
- Cholesterol 32 mg

# Chapter 6: Snacks & Appetizers

## Basil Pesto Poppers

Preparation Time: 10 minutes

Cooking Time: 15 minutes

Serve: 6

**Ingredients:**

- 3 jalapeno peppers, halved and remove seeds
- 1/2 cup cheddar cheese, shredded
- 1/4 cup cream cheese
- 3 tbsp basil pesto

**Directions:**

1. In a bowl, mix together pesto, shredded cheese, and cream cheese.
2. Stuff pesto cheese mixture into each jalapeno half and place onto the cooking tray.
3. Select BAKE mode, then set the temperature to 400 F and the time to 12-15 minutes, then press start.
4. When the display shows Add Food then place the cooking tray in the vortex plus air fryer oven.
5. Serve and enjoy.

**Nutritional Value (Amount per Serving):**

- Calories 75
- Fat 6.6 g
- Carbohydrates 0.9 g
- Sugar 0.3 g
- Protein 3.2 g
- Cholesterol 21 mg

# Delicious Broccoli Tots

Preparation Time: 10 minutes

Cooking Time: 16 minutes

Serve: 4

**Ingredients:**

- 1 egg
- 2 tbsp almond flour
- 2 cups cheddar cheese, shredded
- 2 cups broccoli rice, cooked
- 1 tsp Italian seasoning
- Pepper
- Salt

**Directions:**

1. Add all ingredients into the mixing bowl and mix until well combined.
2. Make small balls from mixture and place on a cooking tray.
3. Place drip pan into the bottom of the vortex plus air fryer oven cooking chamber.
4. Select BAKE mode, then set the temperature to 400 F and the time to 16 minutes, then press start.
5. When the display shows Add Food then place the cooking tray in the vortex plus air fryer oven.
6. Turn broccoli tots halfway through.
7. Serve and enjoy.

**Nutritional Value (Amount per Serving):**

- Calories 322
- Fat 24.4 g
- Carbohydrates 8.2 g
- Sugar 1.1 g
- Protein 17.7 g
- Cholesterol 101 mg

# Meatballs

Preparation Time: 10 minutes

Cooking Time: 15 minutes

Serve: 8

**Ingredients:**

- 2 lbs ground turkey
- 1/2 cup coconut flour
- 1 tbsp fresh ginger, grated
- 1 tsp garlic, minced
- 2 tbsp fresh cilantro, chopped
- 2 tbsp green onion, sliced
- 2 eggs, lightly beaten
- 1 tbsp sesame oil
- 1 tsp sea salt

**Directions:**

1. Add all ingredients into the large bowl and mix until well combined.
2. Make small balls from the meat mixture and place them onto the cooking tray.
3. Select BAKE mode, then set the temperature to 400 F and the time to 15 minutes, then press start.
4. When the display shows Add Food then place the cooking tray in the vortex plus air fryer oven.
5. Serve and enjoy.

**Nutritional Value (Amount per Serving):**

- Calories 259
- Fat 15.4 g
- Carbohydrates 1.3 g
- Sugar 0.2 g
- Protein 32.7 g
- Cholesterol 157 mg

# Crisp Asparagus Fries

Preparation Time: 10 minutes

Cooking Time: 10 minutes

Serve: 6

**Ingredients:**

- 4 eggs, lightly beaten
- 1 lb asparagus, trimmed & poke using a fork
- 1/4 tsp baking powder
- 1/4 tsp cayenne pepper
- 3/4 cup almond flour
- 1 cup parmesan cheese, grated
- Pepper
- Salt

**Directions:**

1. Season asparagus spears with pepper and salt and let it sit on a plate for 30 minutes.
2. In a shallow bowl, mix together parmesan cheese, cayenne pepper, and almond flour.
3. In a separate shallow dish, add eggs and whisk well.
4. Dip asparagus spears in eggs then coat with parmesan cheese mixture.
5. Arrange coated asparagus spears onto the cooking tray.
6. Select AIRFRY mode, then set the temperature to 400 F and the time to 10 minutes, then press start.
7. When the display shows Add Food then place the cooking tray in the vortex plus air fryer oven.
8. Turn asparagus spears halfway through.
9. Serve and enjoy.

**Nutritional Value (Amount per Serving):**

- Calories 186
- Fat 13.2 g
- Carbohydrates 6.9 g
- Sugar 2.2 g
- Protein 13.2 g
- Cholesterol 120 mg

# Cajun Zucchini Slices

Preparation Time: 10 minutes
Cooking Time: 16 minutes
Serve: 2

**Ingredients:**

- 1 1/4 cup zucchini slices
- 1 tsp Cajun seasoning
- 1 tbsp olive oil
- Pepper
- Salt

**Directions:**

1. Toss zucchini slices with oil, cajun seasoning, pepper, and salt.
2. Arrange zucchini slices onto the cooking tray.
3. Select AIRFRY mode, then set the temperature to 370 F and the time to 16 minutes, then press start.
4. When the display shows Add Food then place the cooking tray in the vortex plus air fryer oven.
5. Turn Zucchini slices halfway through.
6. Serve and enjoy.

**Nutritional Value (Amount per Serving):**

- Calories 179
- Fat 13.9 g
- Carbohydrates 11.9 g
- Sugar 1.3 g
- Protein 1.3 g
- Cholesterol 0 mg

# Air Fryer Walnuts

Preparation Time: 10 minutes

Cooking Time: 5 minutes

Serve: 6

**Ingredients:**

- 2 cups walnuts
- 1 tsp olive oil
- 1/4 tsp garlic powder
- Pepper
- Salt

**Directions:**

1. Add walnuts, oil, garlic powder, pepper, and salt into the bowl and toss well.
2. Spread walnuts onto the cooking tray.
3. Select AIRFRY mode, then set the temperature to 350 F and the time to 4 minutes, then press start.
4. When the display shows Add Food then place the cooking tray in the vortex plus air fryer oven.
5. Serve and enjoy.

**Nutritional Value (Amount per Serving):**

- Calories 265
- Fat 25.4 g
- Carbohydrates 4.2 g
- Sugar 0.5 g
- Protein 10.1 g
- Cholesterol 0 mg

# Cheesy Pesto Chicken Dip

Preparation Time: 10 minutes

Cooking Time: 30 minutes

Serve: 8

**Ingredients:**

- 2 cups chicken, cooked & shredded
- 1 bell pepper, chopped
- 1/3 cup basil pesto
- 1/2 cup ricotta cheese
- 1 1/2 cups cheddar cheese, shredded
- 8 oz cream cheese, softened

**Directions:**

1. Spray an 8*8-inch baking dish with cooking spray and set aside.
2. In a mixing bowl, mix together cream cheese, pesto, 1 cup cheddar cheese, and ricotta cheese until well combined.
3. Stir in the bell pepper and shredded chicken.
4. Pour mixture into the prepared baking dish and spread evenly and top with remaining cheddar cheese.
5. Select BAKE mode, then set the temperature to 350 F and the time to 30 minutes, then press start.
6. When the display shows Add Food then place the baking dish in the vortex plus air fryer oven.
7. Serve and enjoy.

**Nutritional Value (Amount per Serving):**

- Calories 264
- Fat 19.3 g
- Carbohydrates 3 g
- Sugar 1 g
- Protein 19.5 g
- Cholesterol 85 mg

# Spinach Ranch Dip

Preparation Time: 10 minutes

Cooking Time: 25 minutes

Serve: 16

**Ingredients:**

- 2 cups spinach, washed & chopped
- 1/4 cup parmesan cheese, grated
- 1 1/2 cups mozzarella cheese
- 1 tsp ranch seasoning
- 1/2 cup red pepper, diced
- 1/4 cup green onion, sliced
- 1/2 cup mayonnaise
- 1/2 cup sour cream
- 8 oz cream cheese

**Directions:**

1. Cook spinach in a pan over medium heat until spinach is wilted. Squeezed out all liquid from spinach.
2. Add spinach, 1 cup mozzarella cheese, and remaining ingredients into the mixing bowl and mix until well combined.
3. Pour mixture into the baking dish and spread evenly. Top with remaining mozzarella cheese.
4. Select BAKE mode, then set the temperature to 350 F and the time to 25 minutes, then press start.
5. When the display shows Add Food then place the baking dish in the vortex plus air fryer oven.
6. Serve and enjoy.

**Nutritional Value (Amount per Serving):**

- Calories 109
- Fat 9.7 g
- Carbohydrates 3.1 g
- Sugar 0.8 g
- Protein 2.8 g
- Cholesterol 23 mg

# Perfect Ricotta Cheese Dip

Preparation Time: 10 minutes

Cooking Time: 20 minutes

Serve: 6

**Ingredients:**

- 2 cups ricotta cheese
- 3 tbsp olive oil
- 2 garlic cloves, minced
- 2 tsp fresh thyme
- 1 lemon zest
- 1/4 cup parmesan cheese, shredded
- 1/2 cup mozzarella cheese, shredded
- Pepper
- Salt

**Directions:**

1. Grease baking dish with olive oil.
2. Add all ingredients into the mixing bowl and mix until well combined.
3. Pour mixture into the prepared baking dish.
4. Select BAKE mode, then set the temperature to 375 F and the time to 20 minutes, then press start.
5. When the display shows Add Food then place the baking dish in the vortex plus air fryer oven.
6. Serve and enjoy.

**Nutritional Value (Amount per Serving):**

- Calories 198
- Fat 14.8 g
- Carbohydrates 5.9 g
- Sugar 0.5 g
- Protein 11.5 g
- Cholesterol 30 mg

# Tasty Cauliflower Tots

Preparation Time: 10 minutes

Cooking Time: 18 minutes

Serve: 16

**Ingredients:**

- 1 large egg
- 1 tbsp butter
- 2 cups cauliflower, steamed and shredded
- 1/4 tsp onion powder
- 1/4 tsp garlic powder
- 1/2 cup parmesan cheese, shredded
- Pepper
- Salt

**Directions:**

1. Add all ingredients into the bowl and mix until well combined.
2. Make small tots from mixture and place onto the cooking tray.
3. Select BAKE mode, then set the temperature to 400 F and the time to 18 minutes, then press start.
4. When the display shows Add Food then place the cooking tray in the vortex plus air fryer oven.
5. Serve and enjoy.

**Nutritional Value (Amount per Serving):**

- Calories 23
- Fat 1.6 g
- Carbohydrates 0.9 g
- Sugar 0.3 g
- Protein 1.6 g
- Cholesterol 16 mg

# Savory Jalapeno Poppers

Preparation Time: 10 minutes

Cooking Time: 10 minutes

Serve: 6

**Ingredients:**

- 10 jalapenos, cut in half & remove ribs & seeds
- 4 oz cream cheese, softened
- 4 oz cheddar cheese, shredded
- 4 bacon slices, cooked & crumbled
- Pepper
- Salt

**Directions:**

1. In a bowl, mix together cream cheese, bacon, cheddar cheese, pepper, and salt.
2. Stuff cream cheese mixture into each jalapeno half.
3. Place stuff jalapeno peppers onto the cooking tray.
4. Select BAKE mode, then set the temperature to 350 F and the time to 10 minutes, then press start.
5. When the display shows Add Food then place the cooking tray in the vortex plus air fryer oven.
6. Serve and enjoy.

**Nutritional Value (Amount per Serving):**

- Calories 218
- Fat 18.3 g
- Carbohydrates 2.3 g
- Sugar 1 g
- Protein 11.1 g
- Cholesterol 55 mg

# Creamy Spinach Dip

Preparation Time: 10 minutes

Cooking Time: 35 minutes

Serve: 6

**Ingredients:**

- 10 oz frozen spinach, thawed, drained & chopped
- 8 oz cream cheese, softened
- 1/4 tsp black pepper
- 1 tsp onion powder
- 1/2 cup Asiago cheese, shredded
- 1/2 cup parmesan cheese, grated
- 2 garlic cloves, minced
- 1/2 cup mayonnaise
- 1/4 tsp salt

**Directions:**

1. In a mixing bowl, add all ingredients except spinach and mix until well combined.
2. Add spinach and mix until well combined.
3. Pour mixture into the baking dish.
4. Select BAKE mode, then set the temperature to 350 F and the time to 35 minutes, then press start.
5. When the display shows Add Food then place the baking dish in the vortex plus air fryer oven.
6. Serve and enjoy.

**Nutritional Value (Amount per Serving):**

- Calories 273
- Fat 23.7 g
- Carbohydrates 8.4 g
- Sugar 1.7 g
- Protein 8.8 g
- Cholesterol 59 mg

# Healthy Zucchini Patties

Preparation Time: 10 minutes

Cooking Time: 30 minutes

Serve: 8

**Ingredients:**

- 2 eggs
- 2 cups shredded zucchini, squeeze out all liquid
- 1 tsp dried chili flakes
- 1/2 cup parmesan cheese, grated
- 1 tbsp Dijon mustard
- 1 tbsp mayonnaise
- 1 cup almond flour
- 1/4 cup onion, chopped
- Pepper
- Salt

**Directions:**

1. Add all ingredients into the mixing bowl and mix until well combined.
2. Make patties from mixture and place onto the parchment-lined cooking tray.
3. Select BAKE mode, then set the temperature to 400 F and the time to 30 minutes, then press start.
4. When the display shows Add Food then place the cooking tray in the vortex plus air fryer oven.
5. Turn zucchini patties halfway through.
6. Serve and enjoy.

**Nutritional Value (Amount per Serving):**

- Calories 128
- Fat 10 g
- Carbohydrates 5.1 g
- Sugar 1.4 g
- Protein 6.7 g
- Cholesterol 45 mg

# Ricotta Dip

Preparation Time: 10 minutes

Cooking Time: 15 minutes

Serve: 6

**Ingredients:**

- 1 cup ricotta cheese, shredded
- 1 tbsp lemon juice
- 1/4 cup parmesan cheese, grated
- 1/2 cup mozzarella cheese, shredded
- 2 tbsp olive oil
- 1 tsp garlic, minced
- Pepper
- Salt

**Directions:**

1. Add all ingredients into the mixing bowl and mix until well combined.
2. Pour mixture into the greased baking dish.
3. Select BAKE mode, then set the temperature to 400 F and the time to 15 minutes, then press start.
4. When the display shows Add Food then baking dish in the vortex plus air fryer oven.
5. Serve and enjoy.

**Nutritional Value (Amount per Serving):**

- Calories 117
- Fat 9.2 g
- Carbohydrates 2.6 g
- Sugar 0.2 g
- Protein 6.6 g
- Cholesterol 17 mg

# Chicken Dip

Preparation Time: 10 minutes

Cooking Time: 20 minutes

Serve: 6

**Ingredients:**

- 2 cups chicken, cooked and shredded
- 3/4 cup sour cream
- 6 oz cream cheese, softened
- 4 tbsp hot sauce

**Directions:**

1. Add all ingredients in a mixing bowl and mix until well combined.
2. Pour mixture into the greased baking dish.
3. Select BAKE mode, then set the temperature to 325 F and the time to 20 minutes, then press start.
4. When the display shows Add Food then place the cooking tray in the vortex plus air fryer oven.
5. Serve and enjoy.

**Nutritional Value (Amount per Serving):**

- Calories 232
- Fat 17.4 g
- Carbohydrates 2.2 g
- Sugar 0.2 g
- Protein 16.6 g
- Cholesterol 80 mg

# Chapter 7: Seafood Recipes

## Air Fryer Cajun Scallops

Preparation Time: 10 minutes

Cooking Time: 6 minutes

Serve: 2

**Ingredients:**

- 12 scallops, clean and pat dry
- 1 tsp Cajun seasoning
- Salt

**Directions:**

1. Season scallops with Cajun seasoning and salt and place onto the cooking tray.
2. Select AIRFRY mode, then set the temperature to 400 F and the time to 6 minutes, then press start.
3. When the display shows Add Food then place the cooking tray in the vortex plus air fryer oven.
4. Serve and enjoy.

**Nutritional Value (Amount per Serving):**

- Calories 158
- Fat 1.4 g
- Carbohydrates 4.3 g
- Sugar 0 g
- Protein 30.2 g
- Cholesterol 59 mg

# Chili Prawns

Preparation Time: 10 minutes

Cooking Time: 8 minutes

Serve: 2

**Ingredients:**

- 6 prawns
- 1 tsp chili flakes
- 1/4 tsp pepper
- 1 tsp chili powder
- 1/4 tsp salt

**Directions:**

1. In a bowl, add all ingredients and toss well.
2. Transfer prawns onto the cooking tray.
3. Select AIRFRY mode, then set the temperature to 350 F and the time to 6-8 minutes, then press start.
4. When the display shows Add Food then place the cooking tray in the vortex plus air fryer oven.
5. Serve and enjoy.

**Nutritional Value (Amount per Serving):**

- Calories 83
- Fat 1.4 g
- Carbohydrates 1.9 g
- Sugar 0.1 g
- Protein 15.2 g
- Cholesterol 139 mg

# Parmesan Walnut Salmon

Preparation Time: 10 minutes

Cooking Time: 15 minutes

Serve: 4

**Ingredients:**

- 4 salmon fillets
- 1/4 cup parmesan cheese, grated
- 1/2 cup walnuts
- 1 tsp olive oil
- 1 tbsp lemon rind

**Directions:**

1. Add walnuts into the food processor and process until finely ground.
2. Mix together ground walnuts, cheese, oil, and lemon rind.
3. Place salmon fillets into the baking dish and spread the walnut mixture on top of fish fillets.
4. Select BAKE mode, then set the temperature to 400 F and the time to 15 minutes, then press start.
5. When the display shows Add Food then place the baking dish in the vortex plus air fryer oven.
6. Serve and enjoy.

**Nutritional Value (Amount per Serving):**

- Calories 361
- Fat 22.6 g
- Carbohydrates 2.1 g
- Sugar 0.3 g
- Protein 40.1 g
- Cholesterol 83 mg

# Delicious Baked Tilapia

Preparation Time: 10 minutes

Cooking Time: 15 minutes

Serve: 6

**Ingredients:**

- 6 tilapia fillets, pat dry with a paper towel
- 1/2 cup Asiago cheese, grated
- 1/4 tsp dried basil
- 1/4 tsp dried thyme
- 1/4 tsp onion powder
- 1/4 tsp garlic powder
- 1/2 cup mayonnaise
- 1/8 tsp black pepper
- 1/4 tsp salt

**Directions:**

1. Arrange tilapia fillets onto the parchment-lined cooking tray.
2. In a small bowl, mix together mayonnaise, garlic powder, onion powder, thyme, basil, cheese, pepper, and salt.
3. Spread mayonnaise mixture on top of each tilapia fillet.
4. Select BAKE mode, then set the temperature to 350 F and the time to 15 minutes, then press start.
5. When the display shows Add Food then place the cooking tray in the vortex plus air fryer oven.
6. Serve and enjoy.

**Nutritional Value (Amount per Serving):**

- Calories 125
- Fat 8.9 g
- Carbohydrates 4.9 g
- Sugar 1.3 g
- Protein 6.7 g
- Cholesterol 24 mg

# Spicy Shrimp

Preparation Time: 10 minutes

Cooking Time: 10 minutes

Serve: 2

**Ingredients:**

- 1/2 lb shrimp, peeled and deveined
- 1/4 tsp cayenne pepper
- 1/4 tsp paprika
- 1/2 tsp old bay seasoning
- Pinch of salt

**Directions:**

1. Add all ingredients into the mixing bowl and mix well.
2. Transfer shrimp onto the parchment-lined cooking tray.
3. Select AIRFRY mode, then set the temperature to 390 F and the time to 8-10 minutes, then press start.
4. When the display shows Add Food then place the cooking tray in the vortex plus air fryer oven.
5. Serve and enjoy.

**Nutritional Value (Amount per Serving):**

- Calories 136
- Fat 2 g
- Carbohydrates 2 g
- Sugar 0.1 g
- Protein 25.9 g
- Cholesterol 239 mg

# Easy Parmesan Tilapia

Preparation Time: 10 minutes

Cooking Time: 12 minutes

Serve: 4

**Ingredients:**

- 1 lb tilapia fillets
- 1/2 tsp pepper
- 1 tbsp olive oil
- 1 tbsp dried parsley
- 1 tbsp paprika
- 1 cup parmesan cheese, grated
- 1/2 tsp salt

**Directions:**

1. In a shallow dish, mix together parmesan cheese, paprika, dried parsley, pepper, and salt.
2. Brush fish fillets with oil and coat with parmesan mixture.
3. Place coated fish fillets onto the cooking tray.
4. Select BAKE mode, then set the temperature to 400 F and the time to 12 minutes, then press start.
5. When the display shows Add Food then place the cooking tray in the vortex plus air fryer oven.
6. Serve and enjoy.

**Nutritional Value (Amount per Serving):**

- Calories 202
- Fat 9.6 g
- Carbohydrates 2 g
- Sugar 0.2 g
- Protein 28.6 g
- Cholesterol 71 mg

# Lemon Dill White Fish Fillets

Preparation Time: 10 minutes

Cooking Time: 25 minutes

Serve: 2

**Ingredients:**

- 2 white fish fillets
- 2 tbsp butter, melted
- 1 tsp dried dill

**Directions:**

1. Place fish fillets in the baking dish.
2. Mix together melted butter and dill and pour over fish fillets.
3. Select BAKE mode, then set the temperature to 400 F and the time to 15-25 minutes, then press start.
4. When the display shows Add Food then place the baking dish in the vortex plus air fryer oven.
5. Serve and enjoy.

**Nutritional Value (Amount per Serving):**

- Calories 368
- Fat 23.1 g
- Carbohydrates 0.3 g
- Sugar 0 g
- Protein 37.9 g
- Cholesterol 149 mg

# Lemon Parmesan Cod

Preparation Time: 10 minutes

Cooking Time: 15 minutes

Serve: 4

**Ingredients:**

- 1 1/2 lbs cod fillets, boneless
- 1 tsp paprika
- 3/4 cup parmesan cheese, grated
- 2 garlic cloves, minced
- 1/4 cup butter, melted

**Directions:**

1. In a small dish, mix together butter and garlic.
2. In a shallow dish, mix together parmesan cheese and paprika.
3. Dip fish fillet in butter mixture then coats with parmesan mixture and place onto the cooking tray.
4. Select BAKE mode, then set the temperature to 400 F and the time to 15 minutes, then press start.
5. When the display shows Add Food then place the cooking tray in the vortex plus air fryer oven.
6. Serve and enjoy.

**Nutritional Value (Amount per Serving):**

- Calories 296
- Fat 16.7 g
- Carbohydrates 1.4 g
- Sugar 0.1 g
- Protein 36.1 g
- Cholesterol 103 mg

# Salmon with Creamy Sauce

Preparation Time: 10 minutes

Cooking Time: 30 minutes

Serve: 4

**Ingredients:**

- 1 lb salmon
- 1 tbsp dill, chopped
- 1 tbsp mayonnaise
- 1/3 cup sour cream
- 1/2 lemon juice
- 1 tbsp garlic, minced
- 1 tbsp dijon mustard
- Pepper
- Salt

**Directions:**

1. In a bowl, mix together sour cream, lemon juice, dill, dijon, and mayonnaise.
2. Place salmon in a baking dish and top with garlic, pepper, and salt. Pour half sour cream mixture over salmon.
3. Cover baking dish with foil.
4. Select BAKE mode, then set the temperature to 400 F and the time to 30 minutes, then press start.
5. When the display shows Add Food then place the baking dish in the vortex plus air fryer oven.
6. Serve with sauce.

**Nutritional Value (Amount per Serving):**

- Calories 215
- Fat 12.5 g
- Carbohydrates 3.2 g
- Sugar 0.4 g
- Protein 23.2 g
- Cholesterol 59 mg

# Shrimp with Cherry Tomatoes

Preparation Time: 10 minutes

Cooking Time: 25 minutes

Serve: 4

**Ingredients:**

- 2 cups cherry tomatoes
- 1 tbsp olive oil
- 1 lb shrimp, peeled
- 1 tbsp garlic, sliced
- Pepper
- Salt

**Directions:**

1. Add shrimp, oil, garlic, tomatoes, pepper, and salt into the bowl and toss well.
2. Transfer shrimp mixture into the baking dish.
3. Select AIRFRY mode, then set the temperature to 400 F and the time to 25 minutes, then press start.
4. When the display shows Add Food then place the baking dish in the vortex plus air fryer oven.
5. Serve and enjoy.

**Nutritional Value (Amount per Serving):**

- Calories 184
- Fat 5.6 g
- Carbohydrates 5.9 g
- Sugar 2.4 g
- Protein 26.8 g
- Cholesterol 239 mg

# Ginger Garlic Fish Fillet

Preparation Time: 10 minutes

Cooking Time: 20 minutes

Serve: 2

**Ingredients:**

- 12 oz white fish fillets
- 2 garlic cloves, minced
- 2 tsp ginger, grated
- 1 lime zest
- 2 tbsp butter, cut into pieces
- 1/4 tsp onion powder
- Pepper
- Salt

**Directions:**

1. Place fish fillets in a baking dish. Top with ginger, garlic, and lime zest.
2. Season with onion powder, pepper, and salt.
3. Spread butter pieces on top of fish fillets.
4. Select BAKE mode, then set the temperature to 350 F and the time to 20 minutes, then press start.
5. When the display shows Add Food then place the baking dish in the vortex plus air fryer oven.
6. Serve and enjoy.

**Nutritional Value (Amount per Serving):**

- Calories 408
- Fat 24.4 g
- Carbohydrates 3 g
- Sugar 0.3 g
- Protein 42.2 g
- Cholesterol 162 mg

# Flavorful Baked Shrimp

Preparation Time: 10 minutes

Cooking Time: 10 minutes

Serve: 4

**Ingredients:**

- 1 lb shrimp, peeled & deveined
- 1/8 tsp ground pepper
- 1/4 tsp onion powder
- 1/4 tsp cumin
- 1/2 tsp garlic powder
- 1/2 tsp chili powder
- 2 tbsp olive oil
- 1/4 tsp sea salt

**Directions:**

1. In a large bowl, toss shrimp with remaining ingredients.
2. Transfer shrimp into the baking dish.
3. Select BAKE mode, then set the temperature to 400 F and the time to 10 minutes, then press start.
4. When the display shows Add Food then place the baking dish in the vortex plus air fryer oven.
5. Serve and enjoy.

**Nutritional Value (Amount per Serving):**

- Calories 198
- Fat 9 g
- Carbohydrates 2.4 g
- Sugar 0.2 g
- Protein 26 g
- Cholesterol 239 mg

# Tender Cod Fillets

Preparation Time: 10 minutes
Cooking Time: 12 minutes
Serve: 2

**Ingredients:**

- 1 lb cod fillets
- 1 lemon, sliced
- 1/4 cup butter, melted
- 1 tsp salt

**Directions:**

1. Brush cod fillets with melted butter and season with salt.
2. Place cod fillets into a baking dish and top with sliced lemon.
3. Select BAKE mode, then set the temperature to 400 F and the time to 10-12 minutes, then press start.
4. When the display shows Add Food then place the baking dish in the vortex plus air fryer oven.
5. Serve and enjoy.

**Nutritional Value (Amount per Serving):**

- Calories 394
- Fat 25.1 g
- Carbohydrates 2.7 g
- Sugar 0.8 g
- Protein 41.1 g
- Cholesterol 172 mg

# Delicious Baked Cod

Preparation Time: 10 minutes

Cooking Time: 25 minutes

Serve: 4

**Ingredients:**

- 1 lb cod fillets
- 1 1/2 tsp lemon juice
- 1 tsp olive oil
- 1 garlic clove, chopped
- 1/2 tsp pepper
- 1/2 tsp ground cumin
- 1/8 tsp ground turmeric
- 1/2 tsp salt

**Directions:**

1. Add fish fillets and remaining ingredients into the zip-lock bag, seal bag, and place in the refrigerator overnight.
2. Place marinated fish fillets onto the cooking tray.
3. Select BAKE mode, then set the temperature to 400 F and the time to 20-25 minutes, then press start.
4. When the display shows Add Food then place the cooking tray in the vortex plus air fryer oven.
5. Serve and enjoy.

**Nutritional Value (Amount per Serving):**

- Calories 105
- Fat 2.3 g
- Carbohydrates 0.6 g
- Sugar 0.1 g
- Protein 20.4 g
- Cholesterol 56 mg

# Curried Cod Fillets

Preparation Time: 10 minutes

Cooking Time: 10 minutes

Serve: 2

**Ingredients:**

- 2 cod fillets
- 1/4 tsp curry powder
- 1 tbsp butter, melted
- 1 tbsp basil, sliced
- 1/8 tsp garlic powder
- 1/8 tsp paprika
- 1/8 tsp sea salt

**Directions:**

1. In a small bowl, mix together curry powder, garlic powder, paprika, and salt and set aside.
2. Place cod fillets onto the cooking tray and brush with butter and sprinkle with dry spice mixture.
3. Select BAKE mode, then set the temperature to 360 F and the time to 10 minutes, then press start.
4. When the display shows Add Food then place the cooking tray in the vortex plus air fryer oven.
5. Garnish with basil and serve.

**Nutritional Value (Amount per Serving):**

- Calories 143
- Fat 6.8 g
- Carbohydrates 0.4 g
- Sugar 0.1 g
- Protein 20.2 g
- Cholesterol 70 mg

# Chapter 8: Desserts Recipes

## Vanilla Cinnamon Mug Cake

Preparation Time: 10 minutes

Cooking Time: 10 minutes

Serve: 1

**Ingredients:**

- 1 tbsp almond flour
- 1/2 tsp baking powder
- 1/4 tsp vanilla
- 1/4 cup almond milk, unsweetened
- 1 scoop vanilla protein powder
- 1/2 tsp cinnamon
- 1 tsp Swerve

**Directions:**

1. Add protein powder, sweetener, cinnamon, almond flour, and baking powder into the ramekin and mix well.
2. Add vanilla extract and almond milk and stir well.
3. Select BAKE mode, then set the temperature to 390 F and the time to 10 minutes, then press start.
4. When the display shows Add Food then place the ramekin on the cooking tray and place it in the vortex plus air fryer oven.
5. Serve and enjoy.

**Nutritional Value (Amount per Serving):**

- Calories 296
- Fat 20.8 g
- Carbohydrates 12 g
- Sugar 2 g
- Protein 17 g
- Cholesterol 0 mg

# Zucchini Chocolate Bread

Preparation Time: 10 minutes

Cooking Time: 30 minutes

Serve: 6

**Ingredients:**

- 2 large eggs
- 1 cup zucchini, shredded
- 1 tbsp cocoa powder
- 1 cup almond butter
- 2 tbsp chocolate chips
- 1/2 tsp baking soda
- 1 tsp apple cider vinegar
- 1 tsp stevia
- 1 tbsp vanilla extract
- 1/4 tsp sea salt

**Directions:**

1. In a bowl, blend together almond butter, sea salt, cocoa powder, vanilla, stevia, and eggs until 2 minutes.
2. Add vinegar and soda and fold into the batter. Stir in shredded zucchini.
3. Pour batter into the greased loaf pan and then top with chocolate chips.
4. Select BAKE mode, then set the temperature to 350 F and the time to 30 minutes, then press start.
5. When the display shows Add Food then place the loaf pan in the vortex plus air fryer oven.
6. Slice and serve.

**Nutritional Value (Amount per Serving):**

- Calories 70
- Fat 4.4 g
- Carbohydrates 4.1 g
- Sugar 2.7 g
- Protein 3.3 g
- Cholesterol 63 mg

# Delicious Apple Muffins

Preparation Time: 10 minutes

Cooking Time: 20 minutes

Serve: 36

**Ingredients:**

- 4 eggs
- 2 tbsp olive oil
- 2 tbsp Swerve
- 1/4 cup heavy cream
- 1/2 cup apple, peeled and diced
- 1 cup almond flour
- 1/2 tsp baking soda
- 1 tsp baking powder
- 1 tbsp ground cinnamon

**Directions:**

1. Add all ingredients except apple into the mixing bowl and mix until well combined. Add chopped apple and stir well.
2. Divide mixture into the 6 silicone muffin molds.
3. Select BAKE mode, then set the temperature to 325 F and the time to 20 minutes, then press start.
4. When the display shows Add Food then place silicone muffin molds on the cooking tray and place in the vortex plus air fryer oven.
5. Serve and enjoy.

**Nutritional Value (Amount per Serving):**

- Calories 37
- Fat 3 g
- Carbohydrates 1.5 g
- Sugar 0.5 g
- Protein 1.3 g
- Cholesterol 19 mg

# Delicious Mug Brownie

Preparation Time: 10 minutes

Cooking Time: 10 minutes

Serve: 1

**Ingredients:**

- 1 scoop chocolate protein powder
- 1 tbsp cocoa powder
- 1/2 tsp baking powder
- 1/4 cup almond milk

**Directions:**

1. Add baking powder, protein powder, and cocoa powder in a ramekin. Add milk and stir well.
2. Select BAKE mode, then set the temperature to 390 F and the time to 10 minutes, then press start.
3. When the display shows Add Food then place the ramekin on the cooking tray and place it in the vortex plus air fryer oven.
4. Serve and enjoy.

**Nutritional Value (Amount per Serving):**

- Calories 207
- Fat 15.8 g
- Carbohydrates 9.5 g
- Sugar 3.1 g
- Protein 12.4 g
- Cholesterol 20 mg

# Zesty Lemon Muffins

Preparation Time: 10 minutes

Cooking Time: 15 minutes

Serve: 6

Ingredients:

- 2 eggs, separated
- 1 tsp baking powder
- 1 1/2 cups almond flour
- 1 lemon juice
- 1 lemon zest, grated
- 3 tbsp Swerve
- 1/4 cup heavy cream

Directions:

1. In a mixing bowl, mix together egg yolks, heavy cream, Sweetener, lemon zest, lemon juice, almond flour, and baking powder until well combined.
2. In a separate bowl, beat egg whites until soft peaks form.
3. Slowly add egg whites into the egg yolk mixture and fold well.
4. Divide mixture into the 6 silicone muffin molds.
5. Select BAKE mode, then set the temperature to 350 F and the time to 15 minutes, then press start.
6. When the display shows Add Food then place silicone muffin molds on the cooking tray and place in the vortex plus air fryer oven.
7. Serve and enjoy.

Nutritional Value (Amount per Serving):

- Calories 204
- Fat 17.4 g
- Carbohydrates 7.9 g
- Sugar 1.3 g
- Protein 8 g
- Cholesterol 61 mg

# Coconut Pumpkin Muffins

Preparation Time: 10 minutes

Cooking Time: 25 minutes

Serve: 10

**Ingredients:**

- 4 large eggs
- 1 tbsp baking powder
- 2/3 cup erythritol
- 1/2 cup almond flour
- 1/2 cup coconut flour
- 1 tsp vanilla
- 1/3 cup coconut oil, melted
- 1/2 cup pumpkin puree
- 1 tbsp pumpkin pie spice
- 1/2 tsp sea salt

**Directions:**

1. Preheat the oven to 350 F/ 180 C.
2. Spray a muffin tray with cooking spray and set aside.
3. In a large bowl, stir together coconut flour, pumpkin pie spice, baking powder, erythritol, almond flour, and sea salt.
4. Stir in eggs, vanilla, coconut oil, and pumpkin puree until well combined.
5. Pour batter into the 10 silicone muffin molds.
6. Select BAKE mode, then set the temperature to 350 F and the time to 25 minutes, then press start.
7. When the display shows Add Food then place silicone muffin molds on the cooking tray and place in the vortex plus air fryer oven.
8. Serve and enjoy.

**Nutritional Value (Amount per Serving):**

- Calories 135
- Fat 12.3 g
- Carbohydrates 3.9 g
- Sugar 1.3 g
- Protein 4 g
- Cholesterol 74 mg

# Vanilla Pecan Muffins

Preparation Time: 10 minutes
Cooking Time: 20 minutes
Serve: 12

**Ingredients:**

- 4 eggs
- 1/4 cup almond milk
- 2 tbsp butter, melted
- 1/2 cup swerve
- 1 tsp psyllium husk
- 1 tbsp baking powder
- 1 1/2 cups almond flour
- 1/2 cup pecans, chopped
- 1/2 tsp ground cinnamon
- 2 tsp allspice
- 1 tsp vanilla

**Directions:**

1. Beat eggs, almond milk, vanilla, sweetener, and butter in a bowl using a hand blender until smooth.
2. Add remaining ingredients and mix until well combined.
3. Divide mixture into the 12 silicone muffin molds.
4. Select BAKE mode, then set the temperature to 400 F and the time to 15-20 minutes, then press start.
5. When the display shows Add Food then place silicone muffin molds on the cooking tray and place in the vortex plus air fryer oven.
6. Serve and enjoy.

**Nutritional Value (Amount per Serving):**

- Calories 159
- Fat 14 g
- Carbohydrates 5.8 g
- Sugar 0.9 g
- Protein 5.4 g
- Cholesterol 60 mg

# Spiced Apples

Preparation Time: 10 minutes

Cooking Time: 10 minutes

Serve: 6

**Ingredients:**

- 4 small apples, sliced
- 1/2 cup Swerve
- 2 tbsp coconut oil, melted
- 1 tsp apple pie spice

**Directions:**

1. Add apple slices in a bowl and sprinkle sweetener, apple pie spice, and coconut oil over apple and toss to coat.
2. Transfer apple slices in the baking dish.
3. Select AIRFRY mode, then set the temperature to 350 F and the time to 10 minutes, then press start.
4. When the display shows Add Food then place the baking dish in the vortex plus air fryer oven.
5. Serve and enjoy.

**Nutritional Value (Amount per Serving):**

- Calories 40
- Fat 4 g
- Carbohydrates 0.5 g
- Sugar 0 g
- Protein 0 g
- Cholesterol 0 mg

# Easy Choco Brownies

Preparation Time: 10 minutes

Cooking Time: 15 minutes

Serve: 4

**Ingredients:**

- 1/2 cup almond butter, melted
- 1 scoop vanilla protein powder
- 2 tbsp unsweetened cocoa powder
- 1 cup bananas, overripe

**Directions:**

1. Add all ingredients into the blender and blend until smooth.
2. Pour blended mixture into the greased baking dish.
3. Select BAKE mode, then set the temperature to 350 F and the time to 15 minutes, then press start.
4. When the display shows Add Food then place the baking dish in the vortex plus air fryer oven.
5. Slice and serve.

**Nutritional Value (Amount per Serving):**

- Calories 80
- Fat 1.6 g
- Carbohydrates 10.6 g
- Sugar 4.8 g
- Protein 8.1 g
- Cholesterol 0 mg

# Coffee Cookies

Preparation Time: 10 minutes
Cooking Time: 15 minutes
Serve: 12

**Ingredients:**

- 2 eggs, lightly beaten
- 1/4 cup erythritol
- 1/4 cup brewed espresso
- 1 cup almond flour
- 1/2 cup ghee, melted
- 2 tsp baking powder
- 1/2 tbsp cinnamon

**Directions:**

1. Add all ingredients into the bowl and mix until well combined.
2. Make small cookies from mixture and place onto the parchment-lined cooking tray.
3. Select BAKE mode, then set the temperature to 350 F and the time to 15 minutes, then press start.
4. When the display shows Add Food then place the cooking tray in the vortex plus air fryer oven.
5. Serve and enjoy.

**Nutritional Value (Amount per Serving):**

- Calories 141
- Fat 13.9 g
- Carbohydrates 6.8 g
- Sugar 0.4 g
- Protein 3 g
- Cholesterol 49 mg

# Chocolate Chip Muffins

Preparation Time: 10 minutes

Cooking Time: 12 minutes

Serve: 6

**Ingredients:**

- 3 eggs
- 1/2 cup unsweetened chocolate chips
- 1 tbsp Swerve
- 1 tsp baking powder
- 1 cup almond flour
- 1 1/2 cups mozzarella cheese, shredded

**Directions:**

1. In a bowl, whisk eggs with shredded cheese until well combined.
2. Add Swerve, baking powder, and almond flour and mix until well combined.
3. Add chocolate chips and fold well.
4. Divide mixture into the 6 silicone muffin molds.
5. Select BAKE mode, then set the temperature to 400 F and the time to 12 minutes, then press start.
6. When the display shows Add Food then place silicone muffin molds on the cooking tray and place in the vortex plus air fryer oven.
7. Serve and enjoy.

**Nutritional Value (Amount per Serving):**

- Calories 293
- Fat 23.5 g
- Carbohydrates 10.5 g
- Sugar 0.8 g
- Protein 11.4 g
- Cholesterol 86 mg

# Berry Cobbler

Preparation Time: 10 minutes

Cooking Time: 10 minutes

Serve: 6

**Ingredients:**

- 1 egg, lightly beaten
- 1 cup raspberries, sliced
- 2 tsp swerve
- 1 tbsp butter, melted
- 1 cup almond flour
- 1/2 tsp vanilla

**Directions:**

1. Add sliced raspberries into the air fryer baking dish.
2. Sprinkle sweetener over berries.
3. Mix together almond flour, vanilla, and butter in the bowl.
4. Add egg in almond flour mixture and stir well to combine.
5. Spread almond flour mixture over sliced raspberries.
6. Select AIRFRY mode, then set the temperature to 360 F and the time to 10 minutes, then press start.
7. When the display shows Add Food then place the baking dish in the vortex plus air fryer oven.
8. Serve and enjoy.

**Nutritional Value (Amount per Serving):**

- Calories 148
- Fat 12 g
- Carbohydrates 7 g
- Sugar 1.7 g
- Protein 5.2 g
- Cholesterol 32 mg

# Chocolate Macaroon

Preparation Time: 10 minutes

Cooking Time: 20 minutes

Serve: 20

**Ingredients:**

- 2 eggs
- 1/4 cup coconut oil
- 1/2 tsp baking powder
- 1/4 cup unsweetened cocoa powder
- 3 tbsp coconut flour
- 1 cup almond flour
- 1/3 cup unsweetened coconut, shredded
- 1/3 cup erythritol
- 1 tsp vanilla
- Pinch of salt

**Directions:**

1. Add all ingredients into the mixing bowl and mix until well combined.
2. Make small balls from mixture and place onto the parchment-lined cooking tray.
3. Select BAKE mode, then set the temperature to 350 F and the time to 15-20 minutes, then press start.
4. When the display shows Add Food then place the cooking tray in the vortex plus air fryer oven.
5. Serve and enjoy.

**Nutritional Value (Amount per Serving):**

- Calories 79
- Fat 7 g
- Carbohydrates 6 g
- Sugar 0.5 g
- Protein 2.3 g
- Cholesterol 16 mg

# Almond Flaxseed Muffins

Preparation Time: 10 minutes

Cooking Time: 20 minutes

Serve: 9

**Ingredients:**

- 4 eggs, lightly beaten
- 1/2 cup erythritol
- 1 cup almond flour
- 1 cup ground flaxseed
- 1/2 cup butter, melted
- 1 tbsp cinnamon
- 1 tsp nutmeg
- 1 tsp baking powder
- Pinch of salt

**Directions:**

1. Add all ingredients into the mixing bowl and beat until well combined.
2. Divide mixture into the 9 silicone muffin molds.
3. Select BAKE mode, then set the temperature to 350 F and the time to 20 minutes, then press start.
4. When the display shows Add Food then place silicone muffin molds on the cooking tray and place in the vortex plus air fryer oven.
5. Serve and enjoy.

**Nutritional Value (Amount per Serving):**

- Calories 259
- Fat 22 g
- Carbohydrates 7 g
- Sugar 0.9 g
- Protein 7 g
- Cholesterol 100 mg

# Hazelnut Cookies

Preparation Time: 10 minutes

Cooking Time: 10 minutes

Serve: 16

**Ingredients:**

- 3/4 cup hazelnut flour
- 1/3 cup Swerve
- 1/2 cup almond flour
- 20 drops liquid stevia
- 6 tbsp butter, softened

**Directions:**

1. Add all ingredients into the mixing bowl and mix until a soft dough is forms.
2. Make small balls from dough and place onto the parchment-lined cooking tray. Flatten each ball using a fork.
3. Select BAKE mode, then set the temperature to 350 F and the time to 10 minutes, then press start.
4. When the display shows Add Food then place the cooking tray in the vortex plus air fryer oven.
5. Serve and enjoy.

**Nutritional Value (Amount per Serving):**

- Calories 92
- Fat 9 g
- Carbohydrates 1.7 g
- Sugar 0.3 g
- Protein 1.6 g
- Cholesterol 11 mg

# Chapter 9: Dehydrated Recipes

## Zucchini Chips

Preparation Time: 10 minutes

Cooking Time: 10 hours

Serve: 4

**Ingredients:**

- 4 cups zucchini slices
- 1/2 tsp crushed red pepper flakes
- 1/2 tbsp onion powder
- 1/2 tbsp garlic powder
- 1 tbsp dried parsley
- 1 tbsp dried basil
- 1 tbsp dried oregano
- 2 tbsp olive oil
- 2 tbsp balsamic vinegar
- 1/2 tsp black pepper
- 1/2 tsp salt

**Directions:**

1. Add sliced zucchini and remaining ingredients into the mixing bowl and toss until well coated.
2. Arrange zucchini slices onto the cooking tray and place the cooking tray in vortex plus air fryer oven.
3. Select DEHYDRATE mode, then set the temperature to 120 F and the time to 10 hours, then press start.
4. Store zucchini chips in an airtight container.

**Nutritional Value (Amount per Serving):**

- Calories 91
- Fat 7.4 g
- Carbohydrates 6.4 g
- Sugar 2.6 g
- Protein 1.9 g
- Cholesterol 0 mg

# Beef Jerky

Preparation Time: 10 minutes

Cooking Time: 8 hours

Serve: 6

**Ingredients:**

- 2 lbs flank steak, cut into thin slices
- 3 tbsp ranch seasoning
- 3/4 cup Worcestershire sauce
- 3/4 cup soy sauce
- 1/4 tsp cayenne pepper
- 1 tsp liquid smoke
- 1 1/2 tbsp red pepper flakes

**Directions:**

1. Add all ingredients into the large bowl and mix well, cover and place in the refrigerator overnight.
2. Arrange marinated meat slices onto the parchment-lined cooking tray and place the cooking tray in vortex plus air fryer oven.
3. Select DEHYDRATE mode, then set the temperature to 145 F and the time to 8 hours, then press start.
4. Store beef jerky in an airtight container.

**Nutritional Value (Amount per Serving):**

- Calories 360
- Fat 12.8 g
- Carbohydrates 9.2 g
- Sugar 6.7 g
- Protein 44.2 g
- Cholesterol 83 mg

# Snap Pea Chips

Preparation Time: 10 minutes

Cooking Time: 8 hours

Serve: 4

**Ingredients:**

- 2 cups snap peas
- 2 tsp olive oil
- Salt

**Directions:**

1. Toss snap peas with oil and salt.
2. Arrange snap peas onto the parchment-lined cooking tray and place the cooking tray in vortex plus air fryer oven.
3. Select DEHYDRATE mode, then set the temperature to 135 F and the time to 8 hours, then press start.
4. Store snap peas in an airtight container.

**Nutritional Value (Amount per Serving):**

- Calories 79
- Fat 2.6 g
- Carbohydrates 10.5 g
- Sugar 4.1 g
- Protein 3.9 g
- Cholesterol 0 mg

# Crisp Green Bean Chips

Preparation Time: 10 minutes

Cooking Time: 8 hours

Serve: 4

**Ingredients:**

- 2 1/2 lbs green beans, frozen & thawed
- 2 1/2 tbsp coconut oil, melted
- 1/2 tsp garlic powder
- 1/2 tsp onion powder
- 2 tsp salt

**Directions:**

1. Add green beans into the large bowl. Pour melted oil over green beans and sprinkle with garlic powder, onion powder, and salt and mix well.
2. Arrange green beans onto the cooking tray and place the cooking tray in vortex plus air fryer oven.
3. Select DEHYDRATE mode, then set the temperature to 135 F and the time to 8 hours, then press start.
4. Store green beans in an airtight container.

**Nutritional Value (Amount per Serving):**

- Calories 105
- Fat 8.5 g
- Carbohydrates 6.3 g
- Sugar 3.1 g
- Protein 1.5 g
- Cholesterol 0 mg

# Lemon Slices

Preparation Time: 10 minutes

Cooking Time: 10 hours

Serve: 4

**Ingredients:**

- 4 lemons, wash and cut into 1/4-inch thick slices

**Directions:**

1. Arrange lemon slices onto the parchment-lined cooking tray and place the cooking tray in vortex plus air fryer oven.
2. Select DEHYDRATE mode, then set the temperature to 125 F and the time to 10 hours, then press start.
3. Store lemon slices in an airtight container.

**Nutritional Value (Amount per Serving):**

- Calories 17
- Fat 0.2 g
- Carbohydrates 5.4 g
- Sugar 1.5 g
- Protein 0.6 g
- Cholesterol 0 mg

# Mushroom Chips

Preparation Time: 10 minutes

Cooking Time: 5 hours

Serve: 4

**Ingredients:**

- 1 cup mushrooms, clean & cut into 1/8-inch thick slices
- 1/4 tbsp fresh lemon juice
- Salt

**Directions:**

1. Toss mushrooms with lemon juice, and salt into the bowl.
2. Arrange mushroom slices onto the parchment-lined cooking tray and place the cooking tray in vortex plus air fryer oven.
3. Select DEHYDRATE mode, then set the temperature to 160 F and the time to 5 hours, then press start.
4. Store mushroom chips in an airtight container.

**Nutritional Value (Amount per Serving):**

- Calories 4
- Fat 0.1 g
- Carbohydrates 0.6 g
- Sugar 0.3 g
- Protein 0.6 g
- Cholesterol 0 mg

# Spicy Pork Jerky

Preparation Time: 10 minutes

Cooking Time: 5 hours

Serve: 4

**Ingredients:**

- 1 lb pork lean meat, sliced thinly
- 1 tsp chili powder
- 1 tsp paprika
- 1/2 tsp garlic powder
- 1/4 tsp pepper
- 1/2 tsp oregano
- 1 tsp salt

**Directions:**

1. Add meat slices and remaining ingredients into the zip-lock bag, seal bag, and place in the refrigerator overnight.
2. Arrange marinated meat slices onto the parchment-lined cooking tray and place the cooking tray in vortex plus air fryer oven.
3. Select DEHYDRATE mode, then set the temperature to 160 F and the time to 5 hours, then press start.
4. Store pork jerky in an airtight container.

**Nutritional Value (Amount per Serving):**

- Calories 168
- Fat 4.2 g
- Carbohydrates 1.1 g
- Sugar 0.2 g
- Protein 29.9 g
- Cholesterol 83 mg

# Easy Kale Chips

Preparation Time: 10 minutes

Cooking Time: 4 hours

Serve: 2

**Ingredients:**

- 1 kale heads, clean & cut into pieces
- 1/2 tbsp fresh lemon juice
- 1 1/2 tbsp nutritional yeast
- 1 tbsp olive oil
- 1/2 tsp garlic powder
- 1 tsp sea salt

**Directions:**

1. Add kale and remaining ingredients into the bowl and mix well.
2. Arrange kale pieces onto the parchment-lined cooking tray and place the cooking tray in vortex plus air fryer oven.
3. Select DEHYDRATE mode, then set the temperature to 145 F and the time to 4 hours, then press start.
4. Store kale chips in an airtight container.

**Nutritional Value (Amount per Serving):**

- Calories 111
- Fat 7.5 g
- Carbohydrates 8.5 g
- Sugar 0.3 g
- Protein 4.9 g
- Cholesterol 0 mg

# Delicious BBQ Zucchini Chips

Preparation Time: 10 minutes

Cooking Time: 10 hours

Serve: 4

**Ingredients:**

- 4 cups zucchini slices
- 3 tbsp BBQ sauce, sugar-free

**Directions:**

1. Add zucchini slices into the large bowl. Pour BBQ sauce over zucchini slices and toss to coat.
2. Arrange zucchini slices onto the cooking tray and place the cooking tray in vortex plus air fryer oven.
3. Select DEHYDRATE mode, then set the temperature to 135 F and the time to 10 hours, then press start.
4. Store zucchini chips in an airtight container.

**Nutritional Value (Amount per Serving):**

- Calories 36
- Fat 0.2 g
- Carbohydrates 8 g
- Sugar 5 g
- Protein 1.4 g
- Cholesterol 0 mg

# Healthy Beet Chips

Preparation Time: 10 minutes

Cooking Time: 8 hours

Serve: 4

**Ingredients:**

- 4 medium beets, peel and sliced
- 1 tbsp salt

**Directions:**

1. Arrange beet slices onto the cooking tray and sprinkle with salt then place the cooking tray in vortex plus air fryer oven.
2. Select DEHYDRATE mode, then set the temperature to 135 F and the time to 8-10 hours, then press start.
3. Store beet slices in an airtight container.

**Nutritional Value (Amount per Serving):**

- Calories 44
- Fat 0.2 g
- Carbohydrates 10 g
- Sugar 8 g
- Protein 1.7 g
- Cholesterol 0 mg

# Turkey Jerky

Preparation Time: 10 minutes

Cooking Time: 5 hours

Serve: 4

**Ingredients:**

- 1 lb turkey meat, cut into thin slices
- 1/3 cup Worcestershire sauce
- 2 tbsp soy sauce
- 2 tsp garlic powder
- 1 tbsp onion powder
- 1 tsp salt

**Directions:**

1. Add turkey slices and remaining ingredients into the zip-lock bag, seal bag, and place in the refrigerator overnight.
2. Arrange turkey slices onto the parchment-lined cooking tray and place the cooking tray in vortex plus air fryer oven.
3. Select DEHYDRATE mode, then set the temperature to 160 F and the time to 5 hours, then press start.
4. Store turkey jerky in an airtight container.

**Nutritional Value (Amount per Serving):**

- Calories 228
- Fat 5.7 g
- Carbohydrates 7 g
- Sugar 5.1 g
- Protein 34.1 g
- Cholesterol 86 mg

# Parsnips Chips

Preparation Time: 10 minutes

Cooking Time: 6 hours

Serve: 2

**Ingredients:**

- 1 parsnip, cut into 1/4-inch thick slices
- Pepper
- Salt

**Directions:**

1. Season parsnip slices with pepper and salt.
2. Arrange parsnip slices onto the parchment-lined cooking tray and place the cooking tray in vortex plus air fryer oven.
3. Select DEHYDRATE mode, then set the temperature to 125 F and the time to 6 hours, then press start.
4. Store parsnip chips in an airtight container.

**Nutritional Value (Amount per Serving):**

- Calories 4
- Fat 0 g
- Carbohydrates 0.9 g
- Sugar 0.2 g
- Protein 0.1 g
- Cholesterol 0 mg

# Dehydrated Bell Peppers

Preparation Time: 10 minutes

Cooking Time: 12 hours

Serve: 4

**Ingredients:**

- 2 green bell peppers
- 1 red bell pepper
- 1 yellow bell pepper

**Directions:**

1. Cut bell peppers in half, remove seeds & cut into 1/2-inch pieces.
2. Arrange bell pepper pieces onto the parchment-lined cooking tray and place the cooking tray in vortex plus air fryer oven.
3. Select DEHYDRATE mode, then set the temperature to 135 F and the time to 12 hours, then press start.
4. Store bell peppers in an airtight container.

**Nutritional Value (Amount per Serving):**

- Calories 38
- Fat 0.3 g
- Carbohydrates 9 g
- Sugar 6 g
- Protein 1.2 g
- Cholesterol 0 mg

# Pork Jerky

Preparation Time: 10 minutes

Cooking Time: 5 hours

Serve: 4

**Ingredients:**

- 1 lb pork loin, cut into thin slices
- 1/2 tsp garlic powder
- 1 tsp sesame oil
- 1 tbsp chili garlic sauce
- 1 tbsp Worcestershire sauce
- 1/3 cup soy sauce
- 1/4 tsp salt
- 1 tsp black pepper
- 1/2 tsp onion powder

**Directions:**

1. Add all ingredients except pork slices into the large bowl and mix well.
2. Add pork slices in the bowl and mix until well coated, cover, and place in the refrigerator overnight.
3. Arrange marinated pork slices onto the parchment-lined cooking tray and place the cooking tray in vortex plus air fryer oven.
4. Select DEHYDRATE mode, then set the temperature to 160 F and the time to 5 hours, then press start.
5. Store pork jerky in an airtight container.

**Nutritional Value (Amount per Serving):**

- Calories 303
- Fat 17 g
- Carbohydrates 3.2 g
- Sugar 1.3 g
- Protein 32.5 g
- Cholesterol 91 mg

# Avocado Chips

Preparation Time: 10 minutes

Cooking Time: 10 hours

Serve: 6

**Ingredients:**

- 4 avocados, halved, pitted & cut into slices
- 1/4 tsp cayenne
- 1/2 lemon juice
- 1/4 tsp sea salt

**Directions:**

1. Arrange avocado slices onto the parchment-lined cooking tray and place the cooking tray in vortex plus air fryer oven.
2. Drizzle lemon juice over avocado slices and sprinkle with cayenne and salt.
3. Select DEHYDRATE mode, then set the temperature to 160 F and the time to 10 hours, then press start.
4. Store avocado chips in an airtight container.

**Nutritional Value (Amount per Serving):**

- Calories 275
- Fat 26.2 g
- Carbohydrates 11.7 g
- Sugar 0.8 g
- Protein 2.6 g
- Cholesterol 0 mg

# Conclusion

The Instant Pot Vortex Plus Air Fryer Oven Cookbook is a complete cooking appliance ability in the market. It is popular due to its large capacity for cooking food and a huge range of cooking functions. Cooking food into an Instant Pot Vortex Plus air fryer oven is easy by just selecting appropriate smart program functions. Instant Pot Vortex Plus air fryer oven locks the flavors and preserves the nutritional values of foods. It cooks varieties of delicious and healthy dishes without adding fats and oil.

CPSIA information can be obtained
at www.ICGtesting.com
Printed in the USA
BVHW010201290422
635713BV00009B/115